AIRSTREAM
AMERICA'S WORLD TRAVELER

PATRICK R. FOSTER

motorbooks

CONTENTS

ACKNOWLEDGMENTS

I'd like to thank Mollie Hansen of Airstream, Inc., for allowing me access to the Airstream company archives and for giving me the opportunity to tour the factory and see for myself how these great vehicles are produced. I'd also like to thank the men and women of Airstream's workforce for answering all my questions as I made my rounds through the plant.

Most of the photos used in this book were provided by Airstream, Inc. The rest of the photos are from the Patrick R. Foster Historical Collection.

DEDICATION

This book is dedicated to a wonderful lady who had a great influence on my life and choice of career—my sixth-grade teacher, Sally Chapin. Mrs. Chapin encouraged my love of reading, always believed in me, and taught me to believe in myself. I've been truly blessed to have known her and to be friends with her today. Thank you, Sally!

Inspiring | Educating | Creating | Entertaining

Brimming with creative inspiration, how-to projects, and useful information to enrich your everyday life, Quarto Knows is a favorite destination for those pursuing their interests and passions. Visit our site and dig deeper with our books into your area of interest: Quarto Creates, Quarto Cooks, Quarto Homes, Quarto Lives, Quarto Drives, Quarto Explores, Quarto Gifts, or Quarto Kids.

©2016 Quarto Publishing Group USA Inc.
Text ©2016 Patrick R. Foster

First published in 2016 by Motorbooks, an imprint of The Quarto Group, 401 Second Avenue North, Suite 310, Minneapolis, MN 55401, USA. T (612) 344-8100 F (612) 344-8692 www.QuartoKnows.com

Motorbooks titles are also available at discount for retail, wholesale, promotional, and bulk purchase. For details, contact the Special Sales Manager by email at specialsales@quarto.com or by mail at The Quarto Group, Attn: Special Sales Manager, 401 Second Avenue North, Suite 310, Minneapolis, MN 55401, USA.

10 9 8 7 6 5 4 3 2

ISBN: 978-0-7603-4999-1

Library of Congress Cataloging-in-Publication Data

Names: Foster, Patrick R.
Title: Airstream : 80 years of America's world traveler / by Patrick R. Foster.
Description: Minneapolis, Minnesota : Quarto Publishing Group Inc., Motorbooks, 2016. | Includes index.
Identifiers: LCCN 2015037894 | ISBN 9780760349991 (hc w/jacket)
Subjects: LCSH: Airstream trailers--History. | Airstream, Inc.--History. | Byam, Wally.
Classification: LCC TL297 .F67 2016 | DDC 338.7/6292260973--dc23
LC record available at http://lccn.loc.gov/2015037894

Acquiring Editor: Darwin Holmstrom
Project Manager: Jordan Wiklund
Art Direction and Cover Design: Cindy Samargia Laun
Book Design: Simon Larkin
Layout: Kim Winscher

Printed in China

On the front cover: 2016 Airstream Flying Cloud.
All images used with permission. All images copyright Airstream, Inc. except where noted.

AIRSTREAM®, the appearance of the AIRSTREAM® travel trailer, and all related trademarks, model names, trade dress, slogans, and logos are owned by Thor Tech, Inc. and are used with permission. Unauthorized use of any trademark of Thor Tech, Inc. or Airstream, Inc. is strictly prohibited.

KING OF THE ROAD

It's the Rolls-Royce of travel trailers, the premier, the finest, numero uno—in other words, the best there is. And, like a Rolls-Royce, it's elegant, luxurious, stylish, and mature. Unlike the Rolls, however, it's an American icon, as patriotic as the flag and as American as its Midwestern home. It's instantly recognizable around the world, eternally beloved wherever it goes. Of course, we're talking about the Airstream travel trailer, the undisputed King of the Road.

Its stunningly graceful lines and pleasing looks have called out to generations of travelers, drawing them to the road and to new lands—and new adventures. In fact, no other travel trailer in the world has ventured so far, so often, for so long, or had more adventures, than Airstream. And no other travel trailer is so universally loved. Once an Airstream catches your eye, you're hooked for life and no other trailer will do. Everything else is just, well, *ordinary*.

That's because Airstream is more than just a room on wheels—it's a luxury apartment, for many the plushest apartment they've ever spent a night in. Airstream has been called "Fifth Avenue on Wheels" because of its urbane charm and up-to-the-minute approach to home furnishings. There's nothing of the quaint or old-fashioned in an Airstream. In fact, the trailer's interiors are breathtakingly beautiful.

This book tells the story of Airstream, something like a Horatio Alger tale of rags to riches, of battling adversity and believing in yourself and your dreams. We'll meet people on the move, Airstream enthusiasts hitting the open road in search of life and their place in the cosmos. Airstream adventures could fill a roomful of books. The Egyptian pyramids? Airstream caravans have visited them for decades, along with the pyramids outside of Mexico City, the sands of Acapulco, the windswept prairies of the American West, and the tulip fields of Holland. Airstream trailers have camped at the Eiffel Tower, the Leaning Tower of Pisa, and the jagged Rocky Mountains. They've also visited the beaches at Normandy, the endless dunes of the African deserts, the sublime loveliness of New England, and the breathtaking beauty of Alaska. Tunisia, Belgium, Canada, Nicaragua, the United Kingdom . . . there is hardly a country in the world that hasn't been host to a caravan of Airstream trailers, because the people who own Airstreams are a restless, adventurous lot. They live for the road.

And, to a person, Airstream enthusiasts have been inspired by the visionary who started it all, a man with a heart full of wanderlust. He took an idea and turned it into an icon.

His name was Wally.

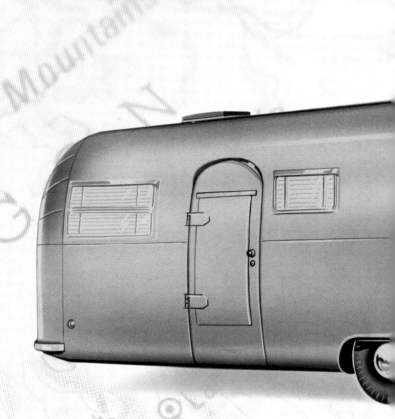

Wally Byam, founder of Airstream Trailers. He stands next to a globe, representing his lifelong goal of opening up the world to generations of travelers via his innovative products and famous caravans.

CHAPTER ONE

MEET WALLY BYAM

Nearly every great product began with a hard-working genius who envisioned it, worried and sweated over every detail of its design, and finally brought it to market. Think of Henry Ford, Henry Steinway, Antonio Stradivari, or visionary duos such as Orville and Wilbur Wright, William Harley and Arthur Davidson, and Charles Stewart Rolls and Henry Royce. These were great men with great ideas, and they worked magic to create products that have unending appeal, products that are evergreen.

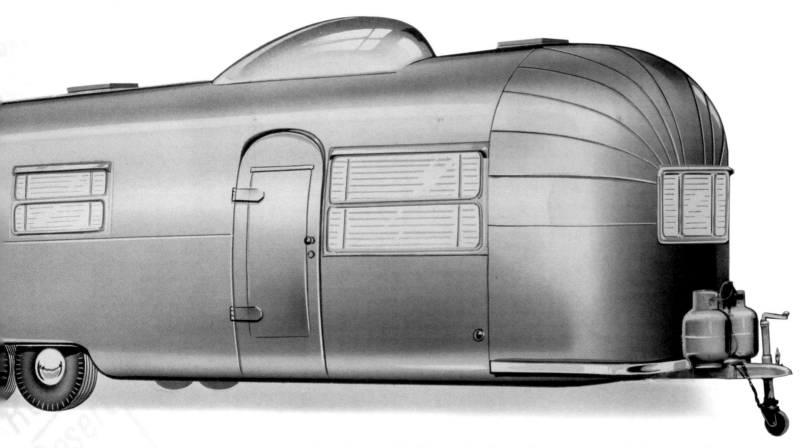

The Commodore, a special Airstream unit built for Cornelius "Neil" Vanderbilt. Chapter 3 covers the story of this unique vehicle.

In the field of travel trailers, one company stands above the rest. Famous for its timeless styling, outstanding design, advanced features, and rock-solid quality, that company is Airstream, its product, the famed Airstream travel trailer. And like those other renowned products, the Airstream was the result of one man's determination to bring a new idea and a whole new level of expertise to the field. His life story illustrates how one ordinary person can rise above humble (even obscure) beginnings and make his mark on the world.

He was born on the Fourth of July, 1896, in Baker City, Oregon. His parents named him Wallace, after an uncle who had recently died, but everyone knew him as Wally: Wally Merle Byam. Even when he was young, people saw something unique in him. He stood out from the rest—an aunt who first saw young Wally Byam standing in a line of third-graders remembered thinking, "I glanced at him and knew immediately that he was someone special."

He came from a broken home, the son of Dr. Willis Bertram Byam, a well-to-do veterinarian, and Carrie Biswell Byam, who worked as a bookkeeper. They divorced in 1899, when Wally was just three years old. For much of his childhood he was shuttled back and forth between his parents, though he remained a happy child.

At the time, Baker City was considered "a hip-shooting, free-wheeling, free-spending, wide-open boom town of the Old West." In other words, it was a rough place.

Wally's mother soon married David T. Davis, a local butcher, whom Wally remembered later as "a Western man—a hard rider." When Wally was nine years old, his stepfather moved the family to Astoria, Oregon, a port town on the mouth of the Columbia River. Wally loved it there—it was an exciting waterfront town with plenty of adventures for a young boy. The port area gave him a place to watch big sailing ships coming and going, up or down the river, often escorted by a tugboat. As a youngster with an urge to see the world, Wally used to dream about where the boats went after setting out to sea. He would later say that, more than anything, he wanted "to go places and see things."

Concerned that Wally would grow up an only child, his parents adopted a girl, Ruby. Since he was a bright child, his mother decided to send him to a Catholic school, where the nuns could offer a better education than what he would get in a public school.

Wally spent his boyhood summers with his Uncle Roger and Aunt Myrtle in Haines, Oregon, about ten miles east of Baker City—another rough-and-tumble western town of that era. In later years, Wally would joke that Haines had seventeen saloons but only four churches!

By the time Wally was eleven, his father had moved to California. Some years later, his father got married again and moved to Idaho; after that, Dr. Byam's contact with his son was sporadic at best. When Wally's father died in 1936, his obituary didn't mention that he had a son.

Young Wally was a clever, resourceful boy, mature for his age. When he was just twelve, Uncle Roger acquired a large flock of sheep and decided that his young nephew was old enough to tend them for the summer season at their pastureland, high up in the Oregon mountains. He set Wally up with a small, two-wheeled wagon pulled by a donkey and topped with canvas for protection against the elements. It was fitted with nearly everything a boy would need to survive in the rough.

With this setup, Wally moved with his sheep to the upper pastureland, where he spent the entire summer. He worked from sunup to just before sundown. Each night, when dark was approaching, Wally unhitched the wagon and propped it up level, letting down the tailgate to provide room for sleeping. The little wagon carried a bed mat, blankets, kerosene cookstove, a supply of food, water, and all the other necessities of life on the range. Through the summer Wally lived and worked alone, accompanied only by his horse, donkey, and sheepdog, caring for his flock and watching out for wolves and other dangerous predators. He rarely saw another human being and spent his time living the carefree life of a cowboy.

This was an invaluable experience that Wally would use the rest of his life: it also gave him the confidence one acquires from learning how to take care of oneself. Sure, it was a rugged life, but Wally enjoyed it thoroughly. "I learned how to camp, how to pack a pack train, how to go anywhere and do anything, and how to care for myself outdoors," he later recalled. It was transformative, showing him a way of living he'd never known could be so enjoyable. Wally always felt his experience that summer helped lead him toward a life and career in trailering. It taught him how to improvise and prepared him to overcome any obstacles he would meet in life.

He was growing up fast and hankered after adventure. Nothing seemed to scare Wally. At fourteen, he spotted an opportunity to ship out with a fishing fleet bound for Alaska. He begged his mother for permission to sign on as a cabin boy, and soon received it, though it must have made her worry while he was gone. His job on board was to keep the captain's quarters in first-class shape, something he did with pride. The following summer, he asked to ship out with the fleet and again his mother allowed him to go. This time, though, he could sign on as an able-bodied seaman, doing a man's job. He was all of fifteen years old and had become a member of the International Seamen's Union, Pacific District.

Meanwhile, his stepfather wanted to move the family again. His business interests in Astoria weren't working out, so he decided to pull up stakes and move to Portland, where he was certain there would more opportunities for them all. Young Wally, now a sturdy teenager, entered Portland's Jefferson High School under a new last name, Davis. Perhaps he wanted the change because he'd seen so little of his real father, or perhaps he did it so people wouldn't ask him why his surname was different from his parents'. Some believe he was ashamed of his real father. Whatever the reason, he changed his name: for a time, he was Wally Davis.

He did well in school, a straight-A student, and he even joined the debating club. It was a happy-go-lucky existence, probably the most enjoyable period of his young life. He graduated in June 1916, a carefree boy with no definite plans for the future.

TRAGEDY STRIKES

As happy as he was following high school, trouble was lurking around the corner for young Wally. His mother suffered from a chronic heart condition. Soon after his graduation, she was taken to Portland's St. Vincent's Hospital for treatment. There she remained, terribly ill for months.

About five months after his mother's hospitalization, catastrophe rode into town. His stepfather's new horse was found wandering in the street, riderless and alone. Recognizing the animal, authorities went in search of Davis. They soon found his lifeless body about a quarter mile outside of town. The horse had thrown him as he was rounding up cattle, and he died from a broken neck.

With his stepfather dead and his mother extremely ill, Wally realized that his life was about to change forever: it was time to get serious. He sat down and compiled a list of personal goals, things he felt he needed to do in order to face his new life.

1. Cease this happy-go-lucky stuff. It's Byamish. [Apparently Wally considered his birth father weak.]
2. Cultivate a memory.
3. Get enjoyment out of the little things.
4. Cultivate willpower.
5. Don't live in the past or future. *Make history*.

Four months after his stepfather's death, his mother also died. He'd become an orphan in less time than

Wally in later life as a travel trailer legend and owner of the best-known trailer brand in the world. Note the many towns and cities he had visited in his extensive travels—Wally was indeed a man of the world.

On tour during the 1950s, a slim and dapper Wally Byam chats with a pair of young ladies.

most have to handle one death in the family, much less two. Wally didn't even have his sister Ruby for company anymore, as she had fallen in love and gotten married. For all intents and purposes, twenty-year-old Wally Davis was alone, orphaned, and completely on his own.

As he himself later recalled, "I was alone in the world. My only relatives were in Haines, and I didn't want to go back there. So I went down to see the high school principal and asked if the school would let me go to Stanford University." They would. But how would Wally pay for it? "I had a little insurance money and sold everything, then went down to Palo Alto and worked my way through Stanford."

HOLLYWOOD BECKONS

The next decision was the biggest: what sort of employment would he seek? Where would he work? Apparently Wally had no thought to use his education to become a historian or a history teacher. He did, however, have some other useful skills. In high school, he'd taken some courses in mechanical engineering, which might point him in a direction.

All at once he got another idea, one that illustrates both his naiveté and the profound confidence he had in his own ability to accomplish anything. Twenty-five years old, Wally decided he would travel to Hollywood and become a famous motion picture director. It's easy to forgive Wally if he appears to have been a little star-struck. This was, after all, 1921, a pinnacle year in the golden age of

YOUNG WALLY BYAM

According to a membership card dated November 22, 1918, from the International Seaman's Union, at age twenty-two Wally Byam (or, as he was known at the time, Wally Davis) was a five-foot, ten-inch tall young man with a light complexion, brown hair, and brown eyes. An able-bodied seaman, he was happy-go-lucky most of the time, blunt and honest. He loved the sea and he loved the great outdoors, and he continued to love both until the day he died.

Wally proved himself a hard worker. During his freshman year at Stanford, he had a paper route and also worked the night shift at the Spring Valley Water Company. He bought a motorcycle to help him deliver papers and to commute back and forth between his jobs and school. During his sophomore year, he was able to get a job with the school newspaper, the *Daily Palo Alto*, selling ad space on commission. By the time his junior year came around, he had become the paper's business manager: at last he had a regular salary. He also became house manager for his fraternity, Sigma Chi.

A thoughtful young man, Wally reflected on himself fairly often, writing in 1917 that, "I am a man of extremes—either I will be a big boss, a rousing success, or a blank failure. In my heart I know I'll be a great big glorious success, and that my name will go down in history."

Wally never took it easy. During the summers he continued to ship out with the fishing fleets that traveled the globe, and, while still in his early twenties, he saw more of the world than most men do in a lifetime. He was growing into a mature, sensible fellow, though he still had all the wild sense of adventure and wonder that he'd had as a boy. He was imbued with a hearty streak of wanderlust.

At some point, Wally wrote another list of personal goals, things he felt he needed to focus on in order to accomplish something good—or even great—in his life.

He saw things about himself that didn't please him and became determined to correct any defects of character. He wrote:

1. Don't be sarcastic.
2. Read good stories—it helps a lot.
3. Become as lovable as possible and let the matter of reward for said loving take care of itself.
4. Become a second Douglas Fairbanks. [In truth, nearly every young man in the country wanted to be like the legendary swashbuckling actor].
5. It's not necessary to commit yourself to a girl to make her like you.
6. When stuck, feel like a deliberate level-headed lawyer.
7. Cultivate a memory.

Like Benjamin Franklin before him, he included tips on becoming a better person in his lists. He was determined to advance himself both materially and socially.

During Wally's senior year at Stanford, he went into business for himself, buying the hot dog and peanut concession at the school's football stadium. He worked hard at running the operation and before long he was, in his own words, "rolling in dough." He graduated from Stanford with honors in 1921, receiving a bachelor's degree in history. His original plan was to stay on at college, in hopes of earning a degree in law, but his restless, footloose nature got the best of him. He wanted nothing more, he said, than "to get out of that place." And that's what he did.

Early trailers were usually boxy affairs made of wood and outfitted with living quarters, but they lacked plumbing and bathroom fixtures. Still, they were extremely popular with folks who wanted to get away from cities and enjoy a stay in the country.

See Page 512

silent films, which saw the release of Charlie Chaplin's *The Kid*, Douglas Fairbanks's *The Three Musketeers*, Rudolph Valentino's *The Sheik*, and Mary Pickford's *Little Lord Fauntleroy*, among many others. America was wild about movies and movie stars, and Wally much wanted to be at the heart of it all. The fact that he had absolutely no training or experience in the field—in fact, *nothing at all* that qualified him to be a director—did not occur to him. A confident Wally packed his suitcase and headed for Hollywood, where he was sure he'd find success.

That golden city of the West was unlike anything he had ever seen. Hollywood was full of glamor, stars, and starlets—as well as thousands of unknown handsome young men and beautiful young women, all trying to be spotted by some producer or another in the hopes of becoming famous. And the city itself was exciting. There were miles of streetcar lines, electric lights and broad boulevards pulsing with people and packed with fancy Packard limousines, big Lincoln sedans, sporty Stutz Bearcat roadsters, huge Duesenbergs, and other exotic cars. Glamorous people packed fancy restaurants and night clubs. Everywhere he looked, there was excitement.

Unfortunately, there was none for Wally. After trying to land employment at a few of the studios, he was forced to take a job as a truck driver to earn his keep. On his days off he continued to canvass the studios for a job, but he had no luck, not even a faint hope of getting in. It eventually proved a hopeless effort. "I didn't even get to first base," he later recalled. Hollywood, it seemed clear enough, was not where he would find fame and fortune.

Determined to better himself, Wally began to scour the Los Angeles area want ads for a job. He figured that, since he'd worked on the school newspaper in several capacities, maybe he could find work as an advertising copywriter; soon he found that jobs were readily available in this field. Then he heard about a new

paper, the *Illustrated Daily News*, that was about to be launched by none other than Cornelius Vanderbilt Jr., great-great grandson of the legendary railroad tycoon. He met with Vanderbilt and, never shy about reaching for the moon, asked for a position as the paper's national advertising manager. He was in luck: Wally and Vanderbilt were nearly the same age and hit it off at once. Vanderbilt (or "Neil," as he liked to be called) hired Wally on the spot.

Wally was innovative as well as hard-working and he did a good job for Vanderbilt. The two built a friendship that lasted a lifetime. After two years in the new job, though, Vanderbilt decided to sell the paper, and Wally was unemployed again. It was time to search for a new opportunity.

Armed with the experience he'd gained working at Vanderbilt's newspaper, Wally had no trouble finding another job, this time with the *Los Angeles Times*, where he sold radio advertising. The job paid well, but Wally hungered for more. As a sideline, he went into business

Travel trailers were all the rage during the 1930s, with scores of new companies producing them for a travel-hungry public. Magazines offered plans for building your own, one of which influenced Wally to enter the business with his design.

Left: Wally looks out from the rooftop opening of a special Airstream travel trailer he built for a friend. A true visionary in the field of travel trailers, and easily the most enthusiastic of the era's travel trailer builders, these qualities have helped his company outlast so many others.

Bottom: A factory-built trailer held together with rivets, lighter yet stronger than old-fashioned construction with nails and screws. Even the early trailers were stylish.

for himself as a magazine publisher, writing and editing for trade magazines on his days and evenings off from the newspaper. His magazines were trade publications centered mostly on the radio industry, featuring titles such as *Radio Trade Journal*, *Radio News*, *Radio Doings*, and *Western Music*, though he was so successful in publishing that he soon branched out into other topics. His magazine, *Game and Gossip*, provided juicy details about movie stars and their goings-on, while *Country Club* covered the world of professional golf even though, as Wally later confessed, "I didn't know anything about golf." He even owned a small advertising agency on the side. Being his own boss suited Wally just fine. "My ancestors did not work for others," he once said. "It's not in my blood."

For relaxation, Wally would camp out in the mountains, enjoying the tranquility and peace that comes with outdoor living. Outfitted with sturdy hiking boots, he walked up mountain trails and alongside mountain streams, drinking in the pure grandeur of nature in all her glory. It was one of the greatest joys of his life.

LOVE FINDS WALLY BYAM

In 1923, Wally met a young woman who knocked him off his feet. Marion E. James was her name, and she was a gorgeous woman with brains to match her beauty—"the rarest combination of beauty and brains that I have ever

seen," as Wally boasted to his cousin. In truth, Marion was indeed a catch: pretty, shapely, and well-spoken, with the refinement and knowledge one might expect from a university graduate. The two soon became inseparable and, before long, Wally popped the question. They were married on June 21, 1924.

In the following years, Wally tried to interest Marion in camping, taking her on trips where they tented in beautiful outdoor locations. Things didn't work out as he had hoped. Despite her reservations about life in the wild, Marion wanted to please her husband; she accompanied him on his journeys, but soon found that she couldn't sleep on the ground. It wasn't all that romantic, and it *certainly* wasn't comfortable. For a well-bred girl like Marion, the lack of sanitary facilities must have seemed appalling, and she also probably didn't care for the mosquitoes, bugs, and critters that campers meet in the outdoors. She and Wally disagreed vehemently about the camping experience.

Meanwhile, Wally's publishing business was going great guns. By 1929, he owned a slate of seven magazine titles—all moneymakers, as America enjoyed the

Top: A photo sent to Airstream by a married couple shows the husband posing with a couple of locals in downtown Tombstone, Arizona. They are parked in front of the *Tombstone Epitaph*, one of the most famous local newspapers in the Old West. The trailer is an Airlite model.

Right: The largest and most successful of the early travel trailer companies was Covered Wagon, with its trademark smooth lines and peaked front-end styling. By the time this brochure was printed, Covered Wagon was using steel construction in its vehicles; though heavy, this offered superior strength to comparable plywood models.

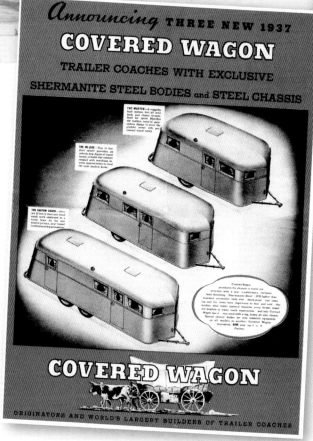

Wally poses with native dancers in Africa during the longest caravan trip he led. Starting from Cape Town, South Africa, the caravaners made their way north to Cairo, Egypt, with scores of stops along the way. The trip took months of travel and required tremendous planning.

Found in the Airstream corporate archives, this photo depicts an early Airstream trailer, probably circa 1933. Although the man is not identified, it appears to be Wally. The early Airstream trailers used this "teardrop" design for aerodynamic efficiency, with the sleeping compartment toward the rear of the trailer. Someone appears to be sitting inside the trailer.

excitement and prosperity of the Roaring Twenties. He and his bride were financially comfortable. All seemed right with the world, even though they didn't enjoy the same things. It was a basic difference of personalities: Wally was rustic and adventuresome, always looking for new excitement, while Marion was quieter and more refined. The two argued frequently about his love of outdoor living, among other things.

If Wally ever hoped to change Marion's ideas about camping, he would have to come up with some new way to make camping more palatable to her. He tried to make things a bit more civilized, purchasing a comfortable wall tent so that the couple would have cots and chairs to sit on while giving them more room to relax.

He later referred to this step as "the dawn of self-containment," the first glimmer of an idea about trailering and the kind of comfort it might later provide. He realized that, for Marion, roominess was a necessity, with space for beds, chairs, kitchen facilities, and so on. In other words, he needed to account for all the comforts of home. For the moment he was focused on tent living, but in due time he would translate these ideas in a trailer of his own design.

Apparently, the new wall tent was enough to mollify Marion, though in all likelihood she never truly enjoyed it. She and Wally were simply different people with different ideas about what constituted a pleasant vacation or getaway. They were still on the ground in the new tent, albeit with comfortable cots. But Marion wanted something better.

THE FIRST TRAILER IDEAS

As he looked for a better solution, Wally recalled the little two-wheeled wagon he'd used as a sheep herder and cowboy back in his youth. Maybe something similar would appease his wife. Building on this idea, he bought a used Model T Ford chassis, which was light and easy to tow. On this he built a sturdy wooden platform, a floor on which he could erect a tent each evening when they stopped for the night. Although this setup was more comfortable than sleeping on the ground, the tent was a pain in the neck to erect, especially when it was raining. Marion didn't care for it, since it was still too primitive for her tastes.

In time, Wally hit on the idea of building an enclosed room on top of the Ford chassis. Two different stories are told about how he hit upon this idea. In the first version, Wally built a teardrop-shaped room on the chassis—a primitive trailer home—that held just enough room for sleeping as well as a small ice chest for keeping food fresh and a kerosene stove for cooking. Wally later recalled a trip he took with this rig, towing the camper behind his four-cylinder Dodge car. "When I got back with this thing it had caused so much comment along the way that I began to think this might be a pretty good business to get into. So I wrote a story for *Popular Mechanics* on how to build one." The readers' response was so strong, he recalled, that he took out an ad in the same publication, offering a booklet of mimeographed plans for one dollar. According to the legend, Wally made more than fifteen thousand dollars selling these plans. Eventually, he raised the price of the booklet to five dollars and provided shop-type blueprints.

In the second version of this story, it was one of *Wally's* magazines that published an ad for building a travel trailer, but the plans were substandard and he found himself swamped with letters from angry do-it-yourselfers who

The irrepressible Wally at a caravan stop in Mexico where he paraded around happily in a large sombrero in place of his trademark blue beret. Byam was part busy manufacturer, part serious businessman, and part showman. His customers and fellow travelers loved him.

had tried to build the trailer but couldn't make the plans work. In this version of the story, Wally decided to try building the trailer himself, realized the problems with the plans, and came up a new set that corrected the defects

A rare photo of the interior of an early Airstream trailer, showing the dinette, dual sinks, and storage cabinets. Note the beautiful wood construction and stylish interior furnishings.

of the earlier plans. He then went on to sell the plans through *Popular Mechanics*, earning a small fortune in the process. At the time, fifteen thousand dollars was enough to buy three nice homes, plus a new Ford car.

Either of these is a good story, but they may be just that. In her 2013 book, *Airstream: The Silver RV*, Tara Cox points out that no such *Popular Mechanics* article can be located. Wally's nephew, however, has several torn pages from the *Autobody, Trimmer, and Painter* magazine dated June 1934. It contains an article titled *Torpedo-Type Tourist Trailer* by Wallace M. Byam that details step by step by step on how to build a trailer. That magazine was a limited-interest publication aimed at body shop owners, however, and it seems unlikely that Wally would have earned $15,000 selling plans to body-shop owners. The true origin of Wally's travel trailer is obscure; it may be that Byam did indeed design the trailer himself and wrote his

story for another magazine, then simply got the magazine title wrong when he recalled it years later. Or, it may be that the second story is correct and somehow got a little mixed up over time. Another plausible theory has it that he saw an ad for plans in some magazine, ordered the plans, and then had to alter them, either to make them work or to conform to his own ideas, thus creating a trailer of his own design. Take your pick.

Whatever actually happened, Wally built a version of the teardrop trailer. In addition, samples of a very early Airstream ad offering either the how-to-build-it booklet for one dollar or complete shop plans for five dollars have been found, so we know that at least part of the story is correct as related. The company listing the plans was Byam Press, 134 South St. Andrews Place in Los Angeles, which was actually the small bungalow that he shared with Marion. The trailer pictured was a teardrop-shaped

One side of Wally's personal travel trailer listing locations and dates of the many caravans he led during his long career. By 1960 this list had grown considerably!

13-footer, advertised as "modern, light, strong." Even at this early stage, it's clear that Wally recognized the benefits of lightweight construction and aerodynamic design. The switch from wood or Masonite to his trademark aluminum construction was years in the future, though.

In late 1929, the stock market crashed, ushering in the Great Depression. With this financial cataclysm, tens of thousands of Americans lost all their money overnight. Some lost their homes and businesses, and many more were plunged into crushing debt. Merchandise sales began to falter and, as economic activity dried up across the country, thousands of businesses were forced to close; others laid off untold numbers of workers. Within two years, millions of formerly happy Americans were queued up in breadlines, begging for handouts, while millions of others worried that they'd be the next to lose their jobs. The song of the day became "Buddy, Can You Spare a Dime?" People began tightening their financial belts and cutting personal expenses.

One expense that was easy for consumers to cut was magazine subscriptions. Before long, Wally realized that his magazine business was in trouble. He tried to hold on for a while, but eventually he had to shut them all down, and then he himself was unemployed. After five years of marriage, Wally and Marion were forced to pack up all their belongings and find a new place to live. Never one to dwell on misfortune, he figured there was always a need for cattlemen and sheep herders, so he and Marion decided to move to Oregon and start all over there.

Wally and Marion still had that teardrop-shaped trailer. Initially, he thought they could use it to make the trip to Oregon: it would certainly save them the cost of getting a room along the way and would give them a place to stay once they got there, at least until they could find an apartment. Before they hit the road, though, that home-built trailer gave Wally an opportunity to earn a living even in the midst of the Depression. His handsome little trailer design had attracted a lot of attention wherever the couple went, and a neighbor finally asked Wally if he would build him a trailer just like it. Always

Folks who travel in an Airstream can see more of the world than those who fly or take the train. Here a traveler observes Sveti Stefan, an island connected by causeway to the mainland in Montenegro, about 4 miles southeast of Budva.

looking for a way to make a buck, Wally agreed. He hired a handyman and they built the new trailer in his backyard.

What happened next surprised even the always optimistic Wally. "[It] was no sooner finished when the fellow next door wanted one," Wally recalled. Then another person wanted him to build a trailer. More people became interested in his trailers and, before long, he and the handyman began building more trailers. Soon the noise of hammering and sawing filled the air in his quiet little neighborhood. Apparently, the construction process made too much noise: before long, some of the other neighbors began complaining about it, so Wally found a small commercial building to rent where he could build his trailers in peace. The idea of becoming a sheep herder was shelved for the moment, though Wally had no idea where this new opportunity would lead.

GOING PROFESSIONAL

Moving the trailer operation from his backyard to a rental building was a big step. It meant he was going from being an amateur builder to a commercial manufacturer. Wally once said he didn't want to run a big mill because that wasn't the sort of life he wanted. But now he would be able to run his own factory, making not raw materials but a completed travel trailer. He was manufacturing something he could be proud of building, which also offered the joys of outdoor living to others. Materially, Wally was stepping out of his old life. He had at last found his place in the world, an occupation he'd enjoy for the rest of his days. Even the calmest journeys encounter a few bumps along the way, and Wally had a long way to go.

The result of Wally Byam's dedication and hard work: the big Airstream plant in Jackson Center, Ohio, where all Airstream trailers are now built. The large building in the foreground is the main plant; the smaller buildings to the left and right are subassembly or component plants. The long, dark blue building left of center is the massive service department and customer waiting area. Across the street is the original bazooka factory that Wally had converted into the Midwest Airstream plant. Today, that building is the assembly area for Airstream's Mercedes Sprinter-based Touring Coaches.

CHAPTER TWO

AIRSTREAM'S EARLY DAYS: 1930–1947

Wally was becoming a full-fledged manufacturer. Opening up a new plant at the beginning of the Great Depression was an act of swimming against the stream, but Wally was unfazed. By now, he was used to doing things his own way. As a man who knew his own strengths and weaknesses, he had long ago decided to create his own luck. Faced with a sickly national economy, starting up a new factory looked crazy, but, as it turned out, he'd picked a great time to launch the business.

Trailer manufacturing was one of the few growth businesses during the Great Depression, and Wally's company got off to a good start. His first factory building was on Motor Avenue in Culver City, California. In time, that facility proved to be too small for the volume of business coming in. Wally soon relocated manufacturing to another, larger building at 22nd Street and Grand Avenue in Los Angeles, near other small trailer manufacturers. Wally started production of his small, teardrop-shaped trailers, dubbed "Airstreams" because they were so aerodynamic that they traveled down the road, he claimed, "like a stream of air." "Streamlining is clean-lining," he often said. Besides, Airstream was the name of the trailers he'd advertised building plans for, so as a brand it already had fairly good name recognition in the industry.

Opposite: Wally's earliest Airstream trailers featured lightweight construction for eaiser towing, along with an advanced aerodynamic "teardrop" shape to enable the vehicle to flow through the air with minimal wind resistance, again for easier towing. The bed was usually situated toward the back of the vehicle.

Bottom: Compare the shape and size of the early Airstream trailers, which were made out of plywood and Masonite, with the lines of this late-model Sport and you can see many similarities: compact size, aerodynamic shape, and low weight.

This mid-1930s Airstream appears in a typically bucolic setting, as families gather to spend some time together under shade trees. This unit has a special art deco paint scheme. It was not uncommom for Airstream to customize each trailer to a buyer's preferences.

These were not, however, the shiny aluminum trailers for which he would become famous: those lay in the future, and he would arrive at their design almost by accident. What he was building now were his standard, wood-framed, aerodynamically styled "teardrop" trailers.

"Remember" Wally once said, "if you want something bad enough, you'll get it—if you work hard enough." As always, he worked hard. The company grew rapidly. By 1932, it was in full production of the Airstream trailers.

Oddly, the more difficult the economic period—the more the country was struggling—the better things seemed to get for Wally's business. Tens of thousands of families had been forced to move from their homes in search of work, and once they landed in whatever town they were headed for, they needed a place to stay. A trailer solved the problem of sleeping accommodations while allowing a freedom of movement that most people had never before experienced. With a properly designed travel trailer, such as an Airstream, a man and his family could follow farm work through the various growing seasons and always have a comfortable place to stay. If his luck ran out and he couldn't find work, at least his family would have a home—one that he could move to the next opportunity down the road.

In addition to this large new "necessity" market for trailers, there was also a sizable traditional market among those lucky few who had *kept* their jobs, who were interested in a less expensive way to travel on vacation. With a trailer, hotel costs were virtually eliminated, dining in became a cheap alternative to dining in restaurants, and picking up and leaving for greener pastures could be a matter of choice rather than necessity.

Even more importantly, camping out had become America's latest fad. Famous people like Henry Ford, Thomas Edison, John Burroughs, Harvey Firestone, Glenn Curtiss, and many others were "tenting out" or caravanning. As the fashion grew, newspaper reporters couldn't write enough stories about the adventures of Mr. Ford and his friends as they traveled and camped. Already, several companies were building and selling travel trailers; one of them, Covered Wagon, was the largest manufacturer by far, with a big plant and mass production. But this was still a fairly young market, and there was always room for innovative newcomers like Wally and his handsome Airstreams. So his company thrived.

There was even a small market for trailers built for traveling salesmen. In these curious products, one part of the trailer served as a home away from home for the salesman, with a comfy bed, sink for shaving, work desk, and perhaps a radio for entertainment. This saved the company the cost of providing a hotel room every night.

The modern equivalent of a vintage trailer would be this 2015 Airstream Flying Cloud, a popular, value-priced model. Note the dual axles and slimline rooftop air conditioning unit.

In the early days of trailering, most campers were grateful to have a dry bed indoors, a sink with a hand pump, and maybe a commode that could be emptied outside. Today's travelers get all the home comforts—and more. Even this 1986 Airstream boasts a full kitchen, comfy private bedroom, bath with shower and toilet, and modern appliances.

The other part of the trailer housed a compact showroom from which a salesman could display and demonstrate his merchandise to prospective clients. It made a unique, interesting, and attractive space from which to conduct business. Smart companies quickly realized how much more productive a salesman could be if he didn't have to waste time trying to find a hotel room, and if he could bring an entire showroom of products right to a customer's doorstep. It made sense.

One thing that set Airstream apart from its competitors was its founder, a true, dyed-in-the-wool outdoorsman who loved trailer living. Wally had caught the camping bug as a youngster, and it stayed with him throughout his life. In fact, becoming a trailer magnate was the answer to a question he'd asked himself many years before, when he faced the dilemma of what to do with his life. "I hate the idea of being a businessman or running a big mill or anything like that," he wrote. "I do not know whether to make myself like that kind of life or become a beachcomber, as in the play. One way gives me success, renown and prestige and the other gives me happiness. Which shall I choose?"

In all likelihood, by the time he was in business for himself, he realized that Airstream let him have his cake and eat it too: he could be a happy-go-lucky camper who just happened to own a highly successful trailer manufacturing company. After all, as owner, manager, and chief test engineer, he would need to make plenty of trips in the trailers to make sure they could stand up to the sort of punishment his customers might encounter. Wally was his company's test driver, product designer, and head of the product development team—and he loved it.

He was also Airstream's harshest critic. He would go on long trips with his personal Airstream; if anything broke, he'd be on the phone with his engineers telling them what was wrong and ordering them to find a way to correct the problem in production. "And don't give me any excuses why it can't be done." He liked to ride inside his trailers while being towed so he could check for air and dust leaks and listen for squeaks and rattles. From time to time, he would also hold "bull sessions" with groups of Airstream owners where he would ask them what they liked and disliked about their trailers. "Have any problems?" he would ask, and whatever troubles they reported would be passed on to his engineers with orders to correct the problem and improve the product. As he traveled around various countries, he would investigate locally made trailers and the companies that produced them, always looking for ways to improve his own products. Over time, he came to appreciate some of the innovative features of English "caravans," as the Brits termed them, and would find ways to incorporate them into his Airstreams. "Let's not change anything," he once said, "let's only make improvements." He followed this philosophy all his years at Airstream.

Wally was often philosophical. "Keep your eyes on the stars and the stars in your eyes," he suggested. "See if you can find out what's over the next hill, and the next one after that." Adventure, according to Wally, "is where you find it. Anyplace; every place. Except at home in the rocking chair." He simply loved his trailering life.

FACTORY-BUILT OR DO-IT-YOURSELF

In an effort to grow the business, Wally decided to offer buyers a choice of options for how they could purchase an Airstream trailer. He offered them preassembled, custom-made units produced in the Los Angeles factory, for pick-up or delivery, or they could buy a build-it-yourself kit that included many of the parts and materials needed to build the trailer, along with comprehensive plans explaining how to complete the construction. As a third option, he sold them an assembly instruction booklet detailing how to build an Airstream trailer from scratch, which he offered for five dollars. This last option was designed to appeal to the most frugal and daring buyers, and to handymen who knew enough about woodworking to actually complete the project.

The first Airstream model Wally's plant offered was a plywood trailer called the Airstream Torpedo Car Cruiser. In this debut model, Wally introduced a new, lower floor, which he built between the frame rails rather than on top of them. His "lower floor" idea was quite innovative, providing greater headroom inside while allowing for an exterior height that was more aerodynamic. "This was a real milestone," Wally recalled some years later. "We were able to install a table with an inset wash basin, a gasoline stove for cooking . . . and even an icebox, in addition to a bed." In time, the rest of the industry copied this idea, as it did many of his later innovations.

Wally tried to manufacture as many Airstream parts and components as possible within his own plant rather than rely on outside vendors to produce them. This reduced costs while allowing him greater control over product quality. Purchasing wood, glass, and Masonite from local suppliers, he constructed the teardrop trailers on frames and chassis he reportedly purchased from automakers, along with automotive-grade wheels and tires. Once the trailer body shell was completed, his workers would begin to construct the interior features: the sink, shelves, cabinetry, beds, folding tables, and so on. Wally's trailers featured large, uniquely shaped windows, side-mounted doors with rounded corners, and hitches of his own design and manufacture.

Wally thought of everything. The uplifted lower rear tail of the trailer (containing sleeping accommodations) was designed to make it less likely that the trailer would bottom out on downhill grades or when exiting driveways while also providing a sleek, modern appearance.

Airstream styling was fully in tune with the art deco movement that was prevalent at the time, which strongly influenced product design in many industries. It featured clean, uncluttered surfaces, aerodynamic shapes, and a feeling of lightness and modernity. The exterior of the trailers could be ordered painted with a single tone, a stylish two-tone paint job, or even—for an extra price—a custom paint design. Nearly every trailer that left his plant was unique in some detail because he built his trailers to customer specifications. To Wally, the customer was king; he considered each a friend and fellow adventurer on the road of life.

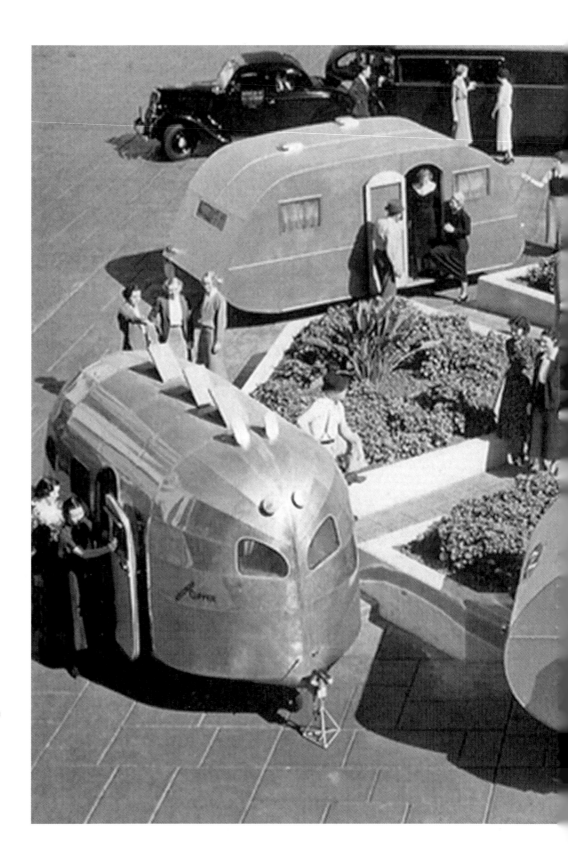

A display of early Airstream models including, at left front, an early Airstream Clipper, the first Airstream model to be made of aluminum alloy. This model is much sleeker and modern looking than other other models. Its rooftop vents allow for good air circulation, while the generous use of foam insulation helps make the Airstream cooler in summer, warmer in winter.

Wally's business grew rapidly. In the middle of 1932, there were reportedly more than 1,000 Airstream Torpedoes on the road, with production continuing to ramp upward. Two years later, Wally introduced a second Airstream model, the Silver Bullet, which was a lighter trailer made of Masonite to reduce weight. This construction made the Silver Bullet trailer easier to tow, even though it was wider than the Torpedo—a design that provided enough interior room for a sideways-mounted bed within its cozy confines.

Being headquartered in Los Angeles provided many benefits for the company, but it did have its drawbacks. The biggest was that Wally had a hard time expanding his sales territory over the entire country. He was probably missing a large number of sales in the Midwest and the East because of his location on the West Coast. He had longed to locate a second plant somewhere in either the middle or eastern part of the country, in order to make it easier to serve the prosperous Midwest and Atlantic markets. It cost a lot to ship a new Airstream to the East Coast, which meant Airstream was losing sales it might

otherwise have made in that region. In California, many buyers could simply drive out to the plant, hook their new Airstream onto the back of their car, and drive away happy. Shipping to buyers located further afield was usually done by driving the product out to them, or hiring someone to deliver it. Either way could be expensive.

Wally continued to produce his small, stylish teardrop trailers, updating them and introducing improvements whenever a need was found. In 1936, the company introduced the fabulous Airstream Silver Cloud, the most luxurious Airstream trailer to date (probably the most luxurious trailer on the road), with interior fittings that rivaled the best hotels. The kitchen galley featured a three-burner stove, a sink with a hand pump, and a lightweight wooden icebox, along with neat countertops. The rest of the trailer's interior boasted fancy curtains and premium hardware, plus silver-and-blue leatherette upholstery for a plush, luxurious look. With the Silver Cloud, Wally was consciously moving upmarket with his products, an especially fortuitous move by the time he made the decision to produce his

The Airstream Clipper was adapted from the rival Bowlus Road Chief, the first aluminum-bodied trailer. The Road Chief offered an advanced design, but poor management drove Bowlus out of business. Wally bought the company's assets, including the tooling for the Road Chief, and set about to improving the design before reintroducing it as the Clipper. Note that the Road Chief's door is at the front of the vehicle; for the Clipper, Wally moved it to the side.

A promotional photo of the 1936 Airstream Clipper. With its sleek modern design and advanced alloy construction, this trailer created a sensation wherever it went. Its aerodynamic shape is reflected in the Lincoln Zephyr towing it.

trademark aluminum trailers. He wanted his trailers to be recognized as the best in the business.

Wally and Marion were doing pretty well financially. They had earlier moved into a pleasant California-style bungalow on South St. Andrews Place (the same address he had used for his plans booklet publishing business), located one block south of West 1st Street. It was a tidy home that featured Mexican-style furniture. Wally insisted on including a bearskin rug, the beast's head filled with snarling teeth, as part of the living room décor, though one wonders what his wife thought of that. Marion's mother Libby and her cat, Marmalade, moved in with them, which must have put a bit of strain on Wally and on his marriage.

THE ALUMINUM TRAILER

Wally was an absolutely tireless worker. Always interested in supplementing his income, he took a part-time job as a salesman at a local Bowlus-Teller trailer dealership.

The founders of Bowlus-Teller were famed aeronautical engineer and pilot William Hawley Bowlus and his partner, Jacob Teller. During his notable career, Bowlus had been a flight trainer, then a pilot for the first regularly scheduled commercial airline in the United States, and later plant manager for Ryan Aircraft in San Diego, where he supervised the construction of Charles Lindbergh's *Spirit of St. Louis* airplane. During a stint in the California desert conducting experiments on gliders, Bowlus had constructed an all-aluminum house trailer in which to reside, rather than make the long trek back to civilization every day. Because he was an aircraft designer by trade, he knew how to use aircraft-grade aluminum, which he combined with advanced aircraft construction techniques. Eventually realizing that he had created a product that was years ahead of its time, he went into business building aluminum travel trailers for the public.

Bowlus introduced four distinct models: the Papoose, Motor Chief, Road Chief, and something he called the Trail-Ur-Boat. The 18-foot Bowlus-Teller Road Chief travel trailer was an exceptionally fine product, a standout in the industry for the time due to its advanced design and construction. Optional equipment included a stainless-steel cocktail bar and an intercom system to connect the trailer with the towing vehicle.

With an exterior skin made entirely out of duraluminum (an alloy of aluminum, copper, and magnesium), the Road Chief featured aircraft-style monocoque (also known as unitized or unibody) construction for the lightest possible weight that also offered exceptional strength. This type of construction combines the body and frame into a single welded or riveted unit that is safer in collisions than separate frame construction and also allows greater interior space. Bowlus's duraluminum body was as strong as steel but weighed only about one-third as much. At the time, most travel trailers were constructed mainly of wood on a steel frame. Industry leader Covered Wagon was using an advanced all-steel body for strength, but Wally could readily see that the Bowlus-Teller product was vastly superior. The aluminum Road Chief weighed a reported 1,100 pounds, meaning it could be easily unhitched by one person; it could even be swung around into position with comparative ease.

The Bowlus-Teller trailer should have set the trailer world on fire. In the business world, however, there's an old saying that a product is only as good as the organization that makes it. As good as the Road Chief was, the Bowlus-Teller Company was unable to market it successfully. Rather than keeping a prudent financial reserve of working capital, the owners overspent on advertising and promotion, and they soon ran out of money. Within a year, the firm was bankrupt, with all its assets sold off at a bankruptcy auction in Los Angeles.

Wally decided to purchase the assets, which included tooling, inventory, and rights to the design. Sensitive to Bowlus's feelings, Wally asked him for permission to take over the company. An understandably unhappy Bowlus is said to have replied, "I neither mind, nor is there anything I can do about it." For mere pennies on the dollar, Wally acquired the best trailer design in the world, along with the special tools and equipment to build it. The Bowlus-Teller Road Chief was destined to become the basis for the new premium Airstream model.

THE BIRTH OF THE CLASSIC AIRSTREAM

With the purchase of the Bowlus-Teller design and equipment, the look and feel of what was to become the iconic "silver slipstream" Airstream trailer began to take shape. Wally hired some of the Bowlus-Teller employees, primarily those experienced in the special construction techniques for building the advanced trailers, and set to work redesigning the Road Chief to incorporate his own ideas.

His first goal was to address design problems. For one thing, the Road Chief's entry door was situated at the very front of the trailer, making ingress and egress difficult. A person had to step over the trailer hitch, which could be challenging, even dangerous, in the dark. In addition, the front-end door didn't allow for what Wally felt was the best floor plan inside.

As his first step in refining Bowlus's design, Wally moved the entry door to the side of the vehicle, the same placement he'd always used on his own designs. This change required a minor redesign of the frame underneath. Always innovative, Wally also installed lightweight Seapak insulation into the dead space between the interior and exterior walls, creating a better insulated, much quieter interior, one that stayed warmer in cool weather and cooler in hot weather, all without a significant increase in trailer weight. This addition was a material improvement over the Road Chief trailer and made the new Airstream more

Another 1936 Airstream Clipper, towed by an older car that appears to be a big Packard. With its well-insulated body and excellent heating system, the Clipper could even be used for winter travel.

comfortable in all kinds of weather. This was an innovation that made the trailer more likely to be used regularly by its owner than another brand of trailer. As a trailer enthusiast himself, that was one of the most important things to Wally—he designed his trailers for people to use as they traveled the country, not admiring their trailer safely parked in the driveway.

In those years, a new Ford two-door sedan could be purchased for as little as $520. The redesigned, reengineered Road Chief trailer, priced at a lofty $1,200, was introduced to the market in 1936 as the Airstream Clipper, borrowing the name of the world-famous Pan Am Clipper luxury flying boats. These large luxury airplanes were designed to travel anywhere and land even where there were no runways. The mighty Pan Am Clippers were one of the wonders of their day, and associating Airstream with them was a clever marketing move.

The Bowlus-Teller Road Chief had been a high-end product, and Wally decided to keep it that way by

building as much luxury into the Airstream Clipper as possible. The new Clipper featured a steel-framed dinette that converted into a bed and fancy electric lights placed throughout the cabin. The Clipper also boasted elegant, cedar-lined closets, an enclosed galley, and full ventilation along with one of Wally's better ideas—dry-ice air conditioning. The Clipper even carried its own water supply, unusual for the time.

Like the Road Chief, the Airstream Clipper was constructed of aluminum alloy sheets riveted to a tubular framework. Although using rivets was more costly and difficult than nails and screws, the latter tended to loosen up and cause rattles and wind noise. To create a larger, more inviting interior, the Clipper had asymmetrical ends with a smoothly rounded front and an aerodynamically sloped rear. The Clipper was large and roomy, with a pleasant interior boasting a row of windows on the side that provided natural light inside while also giving it the look of a modern airliner sans wings.

Top: Wally was interested in helping people find employment; over the years, he provided many jobs to those in need. This photo, taken March 19, 1936, in Los Angeles, California, shows the complete work force employed by the company, then known as Airstream Trailer Company. By this point, the company was starting to grow its reputation as a builder of innovative, high-quality travel trailers.

Bottom: A 1936 or 1937 Airstream Clipper heading out on the road. As an enthusiast himself, Wally believed his trailers should be used for travel, not for plumping down on a lot somewhere as a permanent home. He urged his buyers to go out and see the world.

All in all, Wally's Clipper was a significant improvement over the Road Chief. Its price was certainly an eye opener, but Wally was aiming his latest Airstream at the premium end of the market. Unlike Bowlus, however, Wally had a full line of lower-priced trailers with which to maintain the basic production volume he needed to cover his overhead, so he was able to sell the Clipper at a nice profit and didn't have to try selling them in unrealistically high numbers. His Clipper was a logical addition to the Airstream line, giving people a more expensive model to aspire to and to trade up for.

Wally's new Airstream Clipper created a sensation wherever it went and, despite its premium price tag, he soon found himself with a tidy backlog of orders on hand. As his own advertisements boasted, the new Airstream Clipper was "sleek, dashing-svelte-daringly new, modern in the extreme. It is the ultimate picturization of the streamlined age, so perfect that at speeds above fifty miles an hour the car that tows it uses no more gasoline than it does without the trailer." Even Wally must have been surprised, however, when the president of Mexico, Señor Lazaro Cardenas,

ordered a specially built 22-foot Clipper in 1936. Deciding to personally handle the delivery of the special trailer, Wally and Marion towed it from the factory in Los Angeles to El Paso, Texas, where Mexican government representatives met the couple and took possession of the new trailer. Apparently President Cardenas was very pleased with his purchase; when Wally and Marion visited Mexico City some time later, he made sure that they were entertained royally.

A large part of the new Airstream's undying appeal was the sheer, ultramodern appearance of the thing. Here was the very latest in exterior design, airplane construction, and aircraft aesthetics wrapped around the most luxurious of interiors, all ready to travel the open road at a moment's notice. So sleek, so modern was the Airstream Clipper that it still looks great today. In fact, the family resemblance to today's modern Airstream is so strong that a 1937 Airstream could easily be mistaken for a 2016 Airstream. That's a level of continuity in design rarely seen in a product created for the road. But it's at the heart of Airstream's enduring beauty and attraction.

Taken by the author in 2015, this photo shows a vintage 1937 Airstream Clipper as parked in front of the Airstream Inc. complex in Jackson Center, Ohio. Although the aluminum is faded and a bit discolored, the vehicle remains as rust free as the day it left the factory. How many seventy-eight-year-old vehicles can make that claim? More amazing is how the basic design has remained recognizable over the years—no one would mistake this vehicle for anything but an Airstream.

The market for travel trailers was still young, and, over the years, dozens of new competitors had appeared, but many of them were shady outfits that built substandard units. Working in cramped quarters with day laborers slapping together plywood and Masonite to produce cheap, easy-to-sell travel trailers without regard to quality or durability, the products of these fly-by-night outfits hurt the image of the entire trailer industry. In 1932, when Wally ramped up to full production of his solid, well-built Airstreams, there were just 48 trailer manufacturers in existence in the United States. By 1937, there were more than 400 builders. In comparison, industry-leader Covered Wagon alone produced some 6,000 trailers in 1936, making it a multi-million dollar business. By then there was also an association of trailer owners called the Tin Can Tourists, which numbered more than a quarter of a million members.

Meanwhile, the life of the average trailer owner (or "trailerite," as they are often called) was rapidly improving. As Wally once noted, in the early days of trailering, "if you could sleep comfortably in a trailer, that was a lot. Then, if you could find a place to cook inside out of the rain and wind, that was a big improvement." By 1937, Wally (and others in the industry) had elevated trailering to a level of luxury once thought impossible. Fancy interiors had replaced the rustic simplicity of the earlier days when everything was hand–sawed and homemade–looking, and modern conveniences like sinks, stoves, electric lights, and radios were becoming common, at least in the more expensive lines.

One unfortunate side effect of the move to greater room and comfort in travel trailers was a growing trend by some people who chose to live year-round in their

This 1997 Airstream thirty-foot wide-body illustrates how much of the original design elements have survived over a span of sixty years since the first aluminum Airstream trailers were produced. Although larger and wider, the same emphasis on aerodynamic form and clean, uncluttered styling are recognizable.

trailers—not to use them for traveling. This upset Wally greatly, who noted:

> Something very sad happened. Trailers that were meant for the open road had foundations built under them, never again to travel. Others that did not have actual foundations under them stayed immobile for years on end.

Wally disparaged these contraptions as "trailers in name and legal standpoint only." Unscrupulous builders had discovered that travel trailers were not subject to local building codes, meaning they could be built rather cheaply—especially if they were not meant to withstand the stresses of moving on the open road—thus providing inexpensive housing for people looking to live as cheaply as possible. They could be grouped in clusters on miniscule lots that were rented on a monthly basis. They usually were not subject to property taxes, either—in most cases, owners of parked trailers were only required to pay vehicle taxes. Wally noted that many of them were too big and flimsy to tow very far, calling them "sub-marginal housing built without the restrictions of the building code. They were a disgrace to the industry." Airstream's creed, he declared, was "to never let a foundation be built under one, and never let the wheels stop turning for more than a few months at a time." For the most part, his followers have lived by his advice—on average, Airstream trailers are on the road more weeks out of the year than any other trailer brand. That's because Airstream owners are travelers and adventurers. They yearn for the open road.

Yet, for all its luxury, the Airstream Clipper still lacked a modern toilet, as did other trailers of the day, because nothing workable had been designed. People in the industry had tried to adapt some of the features of boats into their

THE WALLY BYAM CREED

Although Wally never wrote an official autobiography, he did write down many of his thoughts and ideas. One notion he felt a special affinity for was his creed, which he prefaced thusly:

In the heart of these words is an entire *life's dream*. To those of you who find in the promise the words of your promise, I bequeath this creed. My dream belongs to you.

THE CREED

- To place the great wide world at your doorstep for you who yearn to travel with all the comforts of home.

- To provide a more satisfying, meaningful way of travel that offers complete travel independence, wherever you choose to go or stay.

- To keep alive and make real an enduring promise of high adventure and faraway lands . . . of rediscovering old places and new interests.

- To open a whole world of new experiences . . . a new dimension in enjoyment where travel adventure and good fellowship are your constant companions.

- To encourage clubs and rallies that provide an endless source of friendships, travel fun, and personal expressions.

- To lead caravans wherever the four winds blow . . . over twinkling boulevards, across trackless deserts . . . to the traveled and untraveled corners of the earth.

- To play some part in promoting international goodwill and understanding among the peoples of the world through person-to-person contact.

- To refine and perfect our product by continuous travel-testing over the highways and byways of the world.

- To strive endlessly to stir the venturesome spirit that moves you to follow a rainbow to its end . . . and thus make your travel dreams come true.

This creed is still followed today by the Airstream Company.

A scene from the Airstream factory assembly area in Jackson Center, Ohio, in 2005 shows workers hand-riveting body panels, just as they did in the early days. The focus on quality construction remains a big part of the Airstream legacy.

trailers, but, as Wally noted, not one feature had been found to be transferable.

The Clipper did offer sanitary facilities, of a sort. One option was an old-fashion commode with a baked enamel finish for easier cleaning. Another choice was an airplane-type "toilet" placed inside a small box described as looking "like a cedar chest." Chemical toilets were offered by aftermarket sellers, but Wally didn't recommend them, saying, "the only difference between a chemical toilet and one without chemicals is that you just exchange one odor for another." Always a bit of a rustic, he generally recommended the commode-type solution with a bail for easy emptying. He would empty it after every use, often into a small pit he dug nearby. Some trailer models offered a seat toilet that was situated inside the trailer but, lacking plumbing, simply emptied into a hole dug underneath the trailer—not a very elegant resolution.

Meanwhile, the 1936 model year had been a tremendous one for trailer manufacturers, and industry watchers predicted that 1937 would be another year of solid growth for the trailer business. In this they were wrong. That year ended up being a major turning point for the industry, and not a good one. By midyear, it was obvious that industry sales were heading downward at a rapid pace, with no end in sight. Why demand suddenly began to shrink is unknown, but the US economy was still fragile. A sharp, painful economic recession hit the country in 1938, putting further downward pressure on trailer sales, forcing dozens of trailer manufacturers out of business and badly injuring the ones that survived.

Sensing trouble, Wally moved his manufacturing operations to a smaller, less-expensive plant at 2023 West Pico in Los Angeles and soon instituted other operating economies to preserve cash. Trailer sales continued their downward slide, though. By the end of 1938, Airstream was nearly broke. To keep the corporate name alive, Wally continued to register it with the State of California, praying as he did that some sort of turnaround would occur. Things continued to get worse in the industry, however, and more trailer makers went bust. Of the 400 makers operating in 1936, only a handful still survived by 1940.

THE WAR YEARS

Airstream soldiered on through these difficult years, albeit on a vastly reduced scale. In 1940, Wally had to move operations once again, this time to a smaller, cheaper space at 1908 South Magnolia Avenue, still in Los Angeles.

In December of the following year, the Japanese attack on Pearl Harbor plunged the nation into war. Aluminum—indispensable for warplanes and dozens of other military products—instantly became a strategic material. The material was heavily restricted and became all-but-unobtainable for non-essential manufacturing. Wally could still build trailers, but not out of aluminum. He had a chance to manufacture trailers for use as temporary housing for defense workers and the military, but he flatly refused to do so. He wouldn't compromise his core principles—trailers, he said, were for traveling, not as substitutes for permanent dwellings. He would not build them as such.

Lacking the critical materials with which to build trailers and with little market for them other than as wartime housing units, Wally's company went on hiatus for the duration of the war. In need of a paycheck, he went to work for one of the many aircraft builders in the Los Angeles area. These builders had been hanging on by a thread before war clouds loomed over America, but since then they had ramped up production sharply, even before the Japanese attack. The attack on Pearl Harbor, though, focused the entire country on all-out war production, and California's long-suffering aircraft industry suddenly grew

Another vintage Airstream trailer shows the evolution from the earliest Clippers, with a taller body, rounder shape, and a tail that is much less tapered, for improved interior space. Note the stovepipe in the roof and generous window areas.

by leaps and bounds. Wally and all his production workers were able to find employment with no problem, usually at higher wages than what they were earning in peacetime.

Before the war came, airplane production had been an almost crude, homebuilt affair with small companies hand-assembling and hand-painting aircraft, often outdoors in the sunny California weather. Now, with the sudden need to turn out warplanes on an unimaginable scale, new methods and new tools had to be developed to speed up production and ensure greater accuracy and quality control than ever before. It was a great time to be a production supervisor and manufacturing engineer in the aircraft industry and, as an experienced manufacturer, Wally easily fit that role. He found himself in the middle of one of the greatest eras for production innovation in history, watching the development of new materials, new processes, and new tools. As he worked on the warplanes, he noticed dozens of ways he could improve his Airstream production processes once the war was over, as well as new engineering ideas and materials he could introduce into his product line.

Wally worked initially at Vultee Aircraft (which became Consolidated-Vultee in 1943), maker of rugged dive-bombers, then moved over to Lockheed Aircraft, which built the incredible P-38 *Lightning* fighter plane. He later joined the legendary Curtiss-Wright Corporation, where he was employed as a certified manufacturing engineer and production supervisor. It was here that his experience with Airstream really paid off, for Wally knew how to get things built. During 1943, he even taught a class at UCLA on aircraft fabrication and manufacturing methods.

Wally worked steadily during the war years. Like many Americans of that period, he earned a lot of pay and put most of it in the bank, since there wasn't much to spend it on in wartime America. When Japan finally surrendered in 1945, Wally was ready to get back to work on his Airstream trailers. He figured there would probably be quite a large pent-up demand for trailers in the immediate postwar years. He wasn't wrong.

But Wally realized that reviving his dormant company and getting it back into production with the modern tools, dies, and equipment would take a lot of money. To reduce that cost, Wally partnered with an entrepreneur named Curtis Wright (no relation to the aircraft company Curtiss-Wright) to produce his trailers under the Curtis Wright brand name. Originally from Michigan, Wright had moved to California before the war and was now looking for a business that would appeal to the postwar desires of Americans. Like Wally, he figured there would be a significant demand for travel trailers, so they teamed up to introduce a new trailer called the Curtis Wright Clipper. It was essentially the same product as the Airstream Clipper, but with a new name and as many improvements as Wally could incorporate. In time, the Curtis Wright firm would introduce other new models: the Flagship and the Cruiser.

As Wally had noted so many years before, though, his ancestors had always worked for themselves and so would he. Having a partner simply wasn't in his blood, and before long Wally became dissatisfied with his partnership. The inevitable breakup came in late 1946. Wally formed a new company, called Wallace Manufacturing, sharing the same production building with his former partner but building his own Airstream Liner. As soon as he could swing it financially, he moved out of his building and over to a cramped 40x80-foot corrugated metal building at the Metropolitan Airport (later renamed Van Nuys Airport). There, Wally would begin to rebuild his old company and try to reestablish the Airstream name as the premier trailer maker in the country. It was going to take time, money, and a lot of hard work by a lot of people, but Wally was ready. And he was determined.

An Airstream motorhome used as a transfer unit for carrying astronauts from the space shuttle. A long-term relationship between Airstream and NASA began in the mid-1960s when the company produced a specially built trailer to be used for quarantining astronauts upon their return from the moon.

The comfy interior of a 1948 Airstream trailer equipped with twin beds, a popular choice for that period. The fashionable young lady enjoys a cup of tea while reading her favorite magazine. In 1948, Airstream represented the most advanced travel trailer you could buy—and they were popular, too.

CHAPTER THREE

RECOVERING THE MOMENTUM: 1947–1959

Wally had severed ties with Curtis Wright and moved his manufacturing operations into a building at 1755 North Main Street beside the Los Angeles River. It was there that he set up his latest concern, a new business named Airstream Trailers Inc., which became a legal entity on November 1, 1948. Although in name and status a new firm, spiritually it was merely a continuation of the old company. Even after the long wartime hiatus and his reluctant partnership with Wright, Wally's principles had not changed, nor had his core beliefs or his personal creed. Everything prior to this in his life had merely set the stage for what was to become Airstream's future as a world-renowned maker of extremely well-engineered, premium trailers built to an exacting standard and featuring a timeless, iconic design. Wally was now ready to begin resurrecting his dream.

This photo from the Airstream corporate archives shows a family enjoying their vacation in style. The car appears to be a 1948 Studebaker, and it's towing a large Airstream trailer of the same vintage. Judging by the Spanish moss hanging from the trees, the setting is likely south of the Mason-Dixon line.

The new company reportedly bought the assets of Wallace Manufacturing for stock and cash, and under Wally's direction began to produce a line of Airstream-branded trailers. For his initial products, Wally reintroduced essentially the same Liner model that had been built during the Curtis Wright partnership. It was lighter than the old Clipper, as well as easier and less expensive to produce. There were several improvements made along the way. To reduce production costs, Wally decided to use identical front and rear sections rather than the unique endcaps used in the prewar design. This enabled him to greatly simplify the production process and cut hours out of manufacturing time. It also added materially to the available interior space.

The company offered a full lineup of Airstream Liner models, seven in total, each named for a wind:

Southwind Breeze, Tradewind, Chinook, Zephyr, Westwind, Sea Breeze, and a small 16-foot trailer whimsically dubbed the Wee Wind. The Liners offered a variety of interior floor plans and colors, featuring wistful names that included Tender Green and Desert Sand. These trailers were generally priced higher than the competition—after all, high-quality aluminum monocoque construction was a more expensive process than screwing together wooden two-by-fours and Masonite—but most buyers could readily appreciate the difference. As Wally liked to say, "Conversation is cheap and Airstream is not." He knew he had the superior product.

When Wally incorporated the new Airstream company, he was fifty-two years old, a little advanced to be starting up a new venture as ages were figured back then. But deep within himself he knew he really had no choice. Like many people, it seemed as if destiny had planned out his life's work for him, even before he was old enough to vote. Wally realized it himself, once saying that he had "tried to get out of the trailer business several times, but I just can't. Another line is too boring." He was born to build the famous trailer. According to one of his relatives, in the late 1940s Wally had been asked to take over the western distributorship for Volkswagen, an offer he promptly turned down. The relative seemed to think it was a tremendous opportunity, and perhaps in retrospect it was, but it certainly wasn't one that was readily apparent at the time. Other people were offered VW distributorships in the era and likewise turned down the chance. Wally realized that the prospect of trying to sell a small, stark, unknown German economy car with a noisy engine and non-synchromesh transmission didn't seem like a particularly bright one, especially so soon after World War II. In any event, as exciting as Volkswagen became in America, it's doubtful it could have held Wally's attention for very long. He was a trailer man, an outdoorsman, a traveler, an adventurer—one could even say a gypsy. He was not an automobile man. He was born to be a wanderer.

Contrast the 1948 Airstream with this 2002 Airstream Bambi—the similarities are amazing. One of the Airstream brand's many strengths is the continuity of design themes. Like a Jeep, there's little chance of mistaking an Airstream for anything else.

WORKING WITH WALLY

People who knew Wally often described him as a complex individual. He was well-liked by his fellow caravaners as well as by many of his employees. Many saw him as inspirational, driving them to accomplish more than they thought they could. Andy Charles always liked him. Charles came to work for Wally after World War II and stayed for years, recalling once, "He gave me the opportunity—the brashness—to imagine what could be done and, believe it or not, to see it happen."

Others saw Wally as sometimes abrasive. "Don't give me any reasons why it can't be done," he often told his engineers. He knew what he wanted out of life and what he wanted out of his company, and he was not afraid to tell people exactly what he thought. One former worker recalled that, "Wally did not fear expressing his honest opinion whether it bruised someone's ego or not." An executive said, "Wally was a dreamer, and he dreamed big. But he also knew that ideas only have real value when effective action is taken to embody them." A relative once said that Wally had an uncanny way of giving a person confidence to do something he otherwise might not attempt. He was a pioneer who brought about significant changes in the art of travel.

Around this time, after Airstream Trailers had rebooted production, Wally purchased the large, well-known McFaul Brothers trailer dealership to help him distribute and sell his trailers. This association with a popular Los Angeles brand would later prove vital to the growth of Airstream's national dealership network.

At first, what the new Airstream lacked in money it made up for in hope. Wally made sure to staff his firm with men who could get things done. Wally was always loyal to his employees, and they returned his loyalty in kind. One new man, Art Costello, had worked for Wally as a truck driver at Curtiss-Wright during the war. Wally had gotten to know Costello pretty well during that time and realized he was a man who could be relied on to accomplish whatever task he was given. Wally hired Costello to be Airstream's new purchasing agent for materials and supplies.

This was an especially important and difficult job, since raw materials and components were in short supply in the postwar era and Airstream didn't have much working capital to procure what it needed. In the early days, Costello later recalled, the company was a hand-to-mouth operation, chronically short of money to complete production of its trailers. There were even times, Costello related, when employees would dig into their own pockets to loan the company enough money to buy a particular part or component—an oven sometimes, or maybe a refrigerator—in order to complete a trailer and make a sale. While this personal devotion to a production line is atypical for conventional manufacturing companies, there was something about Wally and his Airstream company that made employees want to help out.

Sales had improved to such a degree that, by 1950, Wally realized he needed still more executive help. He turned to Andrew Charles, a graduate of the University of California at Los Angeles who had served as a production specialist at Lockheed Corporation during World War II. Wally knew him from the war years and considered him a talented executive. When he needed help with his growing production volumes, he invited Charles to come work for Airstream.

Left: Wally demonstrating a typical campsite setup with a trailer and an unidentified female assistant, taken around 1949 at the Los Angeles plant.

Below: Taken in Oaxaca, Mexico, in 1957, a young lady guides another through a puddle of water in her 1954 Nash. Traveling in Mexico, Central America, and South America was often quite an adventure because many of the "roads" were unpaved or even nonexistent.

UNSTOPPABLE IN OAXACA, MEXICO, 1957

Charles was shocked by what he saw when he first visited the plant in Los Angeles. Airstream's production processes were primitive in comparison with the frantic yet precise production of aircraft during the late war years. Airstream's North Main Street plant was bursting at the seams to keep up with demand, and some of the production was even being handled outdoors, much as airplane production had been before the modernization brought by the war effort. Charles wanted to get to work streamlining the production process right away, but Wally asked him to learn as much as possible about how the Airstream trailers were made before making changes. He put Charles to work in the furniture-making department initially, then moved him around the plant to see how each job was done. As he noted later, "about ninety percent of the workforce was Mexican," so language barriers could have posed a problem. But, he added, "I spoke some Spanish so I got along marvelously."

Charles was soon straightening out the production process and correcting product defects that were being reported to Wally. With Charles and Costello jointly helping to run the most important aspects of the company, production rose and Airstream prospered. Wally continued building a solid dealer network to sell and service a growing cadre of loyal Airstream owners. By 1950, the company was solidly profitable. Wally was increasingly anxious to go out on the road: at an age when many men

"I've been in the trucking business for 30 years...I go Airstream"

Says Joe Bos, Bos Truck Lines, Marshalltown, Iowa

"You can't operate a fleet of over-the-highway trucks for more than a quarter century without learning a little about what makes a good rig for the road. Design, construction and attention to details are important to any unit that has to take the abuse of towing. My Airstream is tops in all those departments and has every requirement for luxury living, too. Airstream's combination is unbeatable."

Mr. Bos has proven his Airstream on the roads of Europe, Mexico, Central America and the United States and he has enjoyed the comfortable freedom provided by Airstream's many self-containment features ... the marvelous developments that permit you to stop in out-of-the-way places and to live in the same style you would at home: Electricity, hot and cold running water, refrigeration, bathroom, superb beds and the kitchen of your dreams with no outside connections. Airstream's combination *is* unbeatable for those with the spirit of travel-adventure.

JOIN ONE OF WALLY BYAM'S EXCITING AIRSTREAM CARAVANS

Joe Bos was a man who knew how to spot quality in an over-the-road vehicle; according to this ad, he operated a fleet of big trucks for over twenty-five years. And, knowing quality, he chose Airstream for his personal use.

retire, he was full of energy and dreams. In many ways, the 1950s would be the most exciting part of his life.

The company introduced a new Airstream model for 1951, the Flying Cloud. It was a contemporary, handsome take on the classic Airstream design, a 21-footer that featured a modern ladder frame, a unique A-frame tongue hitch, and front and rear caps that were flattened out a bit to improve interior space. Wally liked to brag that, like other Airstream trailers, the new Flying Cloud was manufactured on airplane-style jigs, with aircraft-style construction techniques and airplane-grade aluminum alloys. The new Flying Cloud joined the growing lineup of Airstream trailers, including the 24-foot Cruiser, 32-foot Liner, and 18-foot Clipper.

THE FIRST BIG CARAVAN TO MEXICO

Wally had already done quite a bit of traveling in his personal Airstream trailer—he'd journeyed to Mexico, Northern California, the American West, and many other locations in North America. He'd even gone on a grand tour of Europe with his old friend Neil Vanderbilt in 1948.

Now he was looking for something grander—rather than travel alone, Wally decided that he wanted to take a trip with some friends in a caravan-style tour of Mexico. It would be a sort of modern "wagon train," circa 1951. Wally initially envisioned about four trailers traveling together on the trip.

The plan expanded from that humble original vision. It started when a trailer enthusiast magazine heard about the proposed caravan and mentioned it in one of their issues, after which several readers asked Wally if they could come along in their own trailers. Wally agreed. Always on the lookout for promotional opportunities, he placed an ad in the *Los Angeles Times* with the announcement that he and several friends would soon travel via caravan to Mexico—and also Nicaragua. Furthermore, he offered places in his caravan for any intrepid trailer owners who were willing to pay a $316 entry fee. Overnight, his plan had grown from a straightforward trip to Mexico to what could easily prove to be a long and arduous expedition deep into Central America. Wally was dreaming really big this time.

In later accounts, he said that he expected a fairly good turnout from his ad, maybe thirty-five trailers. The most quoted version of the story holds that a total *sixty-three trailers* converged on the assembly point near the border crossing at El Paso, Texas, on December 1, 1951. Not all of them were even Airstreams. Every kind of tow car was represented—big Nashes, Buicks, Chevies, and Fords, along with Cadillacs, and even a Jeep. The trailer owners themselves included doctors, teachers, millionaires, farmers, and bankers—folks from all walks of life, with a broad range of travel experience. Although most were familiar with trailering, none had taken a trailer journey this far away from home. Despite the distances involved, though, all were inspired by Wally's enthusiasm, and they all wanted to take to the road with him in search of fun and adventure. They were ready to roll.

Sometime before the caravan to Mexico, Wally and Marion's marriage finally came to an end. Once they had really been in love, but that was years ago. Wally was now seeing a woman named Estelle Hall, known to everyone as Stella. People who saw them together felt they were the perfect couple, both enjoying good times and good company and both born with an adventurous spirit. Like Wally, Stella enjoyed the great outdoors and the idea of traveling to exotic places. She decided to go along on the Mexico trip, Wally's first large-scale caravan. It sounded like great fun to her, and she even invited her mother to come along. Wally was ecstatic that Stella was joining the group.

He brought along a guest as well. Although he and Marion had had no children, Wally had formed a friendship with his young second cousin, a twelve-year-old boy named Dale Schwamborn, whom he nicknamed Pee Wee. Wally invited him to join the adventure, and Pee Wee happily accepted.

With Wally in charge, as the "Wagonmaster," the hardy travelers set out on a journey that would serve as a learning experience for everyone involved. No one had ever attempted so ambitious a trip via modern caravan, at least not on the scale of Wally's expedition.

The journey lasted a total of four months. It proved much more difficult than anyone had imagined, not

In 1952 Cornelius Vanderbilt and Wally Byam decided to take a road trip. The two traveled to Chicago, where Vanderbilt would cover the Democratic and Republican conventions as a journalist. Wally went along, too, planning to continue on a tour of the Midwest in search of a suitable building for his new factory. Andy Charles, who would manage the plant, also went along.

least because of the bad roads in Mexico and those in Central America that were even worse or nonexistent. Many of the so-called "roads" the travelers were forced to take were nearly impassable, and at several points each trailer-and-car combination had to be helped along through potholes, mud holes, over large rocks and boulders, through treacherous overgrown vegetation, and through rough patches where the pavement was nothing but ruts, rocks, and stones. The travelers' cars suffered all kinds of road-related troubles, including tire failures (on both cars and trailers), blown transmissions and clutches, broken springs, broken axles, and worn-out brakes. With each obstacle or breakdown, the caravan was forced to stop and help their fellow travelers, and often the entire caravan of trailers had to halt until repair parts could be found and a capable mechanic could make the needed repairs.

There were weather-related problems, too—blazing-hot days that caused cars to overheat, torrential rains that washed out the poor roads and halted the procession until they were clear. In short there was, as Wally put it,

"every disaster you can imagine." As the days and weeks wore on, many of the travelers became discouraged and turned back, while others became so disgusted that they sold their trailers on the spot and flew home via commercial airplane. By the time the worn and battered caravan—"a bedraggled lot," as Wally put it—made their way back to the United States, the group had shrunk to just fourteen trailers and their owners, all of them hale and hardy survivors of what was in all likelihood the greatest journey of their lifetimes. Even the usually indefatigable Wally had become discouraged, and why not? He had been the point man that everyone turned to when they had a problem, and they had a host of problems on the trip. Over the four-month period, Wally lost twenty seven pounds while gaining, as he noted, "a new outcropping of gray hair." He vowed never to attempt to lead another such trip as long as he lived.

Fortunately for the travel trailer industry, though, the one thing Wally Byam couldn't do was stop being Wally Byam. He had been born with a wandering heart, and he wouldn't stop exploring until that heart stopped beating.

Perhaps he sincerely believed it when he said he'd never lead another big caravan again, but the fact is that, a year after the Central American misadventure of 1951–1952, Wally was planning another big trip. He couldn't help it—the lure of the road had him in its grip. He had to keep moving, keep searching for new adventures.

For 1953, then, Wally organized another caravan. This time they would travel a shorter distance and (they hoped) encounter fewer worries along the way, as well as less wear and tear on all concerned. For this second big caravan of the 1950s, he would lead a group of thirty-eight trailers and their inhabitants down the west coast of Mexico to sunny Acapulco, one of the great hot spots of the decade. It was a well-loved resort town for many Hollywood movie stars and wannabes.

The journey to Acapulco went surprisingly well. Wally put what he'd learned on his first trip to good use for the second. In later years, Wally would lead another five caravans to Mexico, five others to Canada, two more to Central America—by this point, he figured he'd learned

The sophisticated "Neil" Vanderbilt greets Mr. and Mrs. Mike Wallace in Chicago during the Midwest trip he and Wally took in 1952.

the ropes—plus Yellowstone National Park and a highly adventurous trip to Cuba. He would also undertake a six-month grand tour of Europe via caravan. Then, in 1959, he made his greatest trip ever when he led a group of brave souls on an 18,000-mile trek from the salty shores of Cape Town, South Africa, to the arid sand dunes of Cairo, Egypt.

A GROWING CONTROVERSY— AND A NEW PLANT

Airstream continued to grow. With Wally on the road for months at a time, it fell to Costello and Charles to actually run Airstream Trailers, Inc. Costello focused his energies on running the day-to-day details of the business, as well as handling labor relations. A gregarious man, usually dressed in flashy clothes, he could be utterly charming at times, and stubborn, quick-tempered and difficult at others. He was known as a tough-minded businessman and not a person to cross.

Charles was practically his polar opposite. A serious, contemplative man, he was considered well-read, perhaps even a bit of an intellectual, with interests including books, cuisine, and world travel. As befits a person with such interests, Charles's domain was product design and sales.

Wally put the men in charge of separate aspects of the business, in hopes that they would complement each other. He always urged cooperation in his plants because Airstream was a small company and, if it had any hope of being successful, it needed everyone to work together. Regular employees generally did follow that direction. Nevertheless, when a person enters a management role, he or she often goes through a personality change. Having gained a little power, such a person soon desires more and more. This seems to be what happened with Costello and, to a lesser extent, Charles. A power struggle grew between them: both men, probably realizing that Wally would retire in the next decade, silently fought each other, all the while seeking favor from the boss and eventual control of the company. Each tried to undermine the other's efforts. This was not a constructive, or sustainable, situation.

In 1952, downtown Jackson Center, Ohio, was hardly a bustling hub of activity. This small midwestern town was far from the big cities, but its closed-down factory caught the eye of Wally Byam and Andy Charles. They decided it would make a great second plant for Airstream, so Wally bought it and began preparing it for trailer production.

Wally finally came up with what he thought was the right cure for the problem—he would give each man a plant to run. As business continued to improve, he had decided it was time to realize an old, long-held dream of his—to open a second Airstream plant that could better serve markets in the eastern half of the United States. At the same time, this plan would give each of his top lieutenants a factory they could run essentially as their own business, and peace—hopefully—would reign within the Airstream family.

Wally's initial planning was fairly simple. He knew a cluster of travel trailer businesses was situated in Elkhart, Indiana, along with related supplier plants that made interior fittings, fixtures, appliances, and components, and his plant should be located a reasonable distance from them so he could use them

as suppliers. By doing so, he could save a great deal of time and trouble as he set up a supplier base for the new plant. He wanted to situate his new factory in the Midwest because of its ready supply of skilled and unskilled labor and the availability of relatively inexpensive land. Lastly, he knew that a number of small plants had been erected during the war years to build specific military products; these were now lying dormant. Wally hoped he could find one that was the right size for his planned new manufacturing center.

But here Wally's sometimes flighty way of doing things took over. Where the plant should be? Indiana, Michigan, Illinois, and Ohio were all possibilities. But rather than hire a commercial realtor to seek possible factory sites, Wally and Charles simply hit the road in a specially built fiberglass

Airstream trailer with Vanderbilt, going in search of the next Airstream factory location. It would essentially be one big road trip with no map and little direction.

The special 33-foot blue and white Airstream trailer they used was a marvel of modern living, and was equipped with a bar, television set, two bathrooms, and a library—it even boasted two-way radiophones. The custom interior was styled by a popular interior designer of the day, Charles Criqui. Dubbed the Commodore, this highly sophisticated experimental trailer was built by Airstream at a time when Wally was considering fiberglass as a building material for his trailers. Fiberglass was strong and even lighter than aluminum. The plan was for Wally, Charles, and Vanderbilt to tow the plastic Commodore to Chicago, where Vanderbilt planned to write about the 1952 Democratic and Republican national conventions. While in Chicago, the idea went, they could host cocktail parties and receptions in the trailer, gaining a huge amount of publicity for Airstream products.

Upon arriving in Chicago they parked the glamorous Commodore on the green near the Hotel Ambassador West and proceeded to carry out a round of cocktail parties and receptions that attracted hundreds of influential people. A total of 382 persons signed the guest book, and the list of dignitaries that attended the parties included twenty-two senators, sixteen governors, and many journalists (including a young journalist named Mike Wallace, later of *60 Minutes* fame), as well as several members of the House of Representatives. All of them were wined and dined, and most of them, it's safe to assume, were highly impressed by the Commodore. Who wouldn't be?

Wally and Charles left Chicago in the tow car they had brought, a sturdy 1952 Chevrolet Suburban wagon, while Vanderbilt stayed behind in the Commodore trailer to entertain, to party, and perhaps even to write about the conventions as originally planned.

Wally and Charles set out on the road in search of a suitable plant for Airstream. Throughout the drive, Wally was in pain. At a farewell party just before leaving Los Angeles, he'd stepped off a table (probably showing off)

and broken a bone in his foot. To ease the pain, the CEO of one of the foremost trailer companies in the world removed his sock and hung his sore foot out the window as Charles drove the Chevy down the highway. They motored through Illinois and on to Dayton, Ohio, stopping there to visit one of Wally's cousins. The next day, they continued on to Sidney, Ohio, a small town in Shelby County, deep in farming country. At the local chamber of commerce, Wally and Charles asked about commercial buildings that were for sale in the area. They were told that an empty plant was available in nearby Jackson Center, a tiny farming community 15 miles to the northeast.

THE BAZOOKA PLANT

Despite the late hour, the two men drove out to see the place. It was a sturdy steel building erected during the war to produce bazookas for the army. Now the structure was empty, dusty, dirty, and completely abandoned in the midst of a sea of 6-foot-tall weeds. With his foot aching, Wally begged off tromping through the weeds to look at the derelict factory. On his own, Charles went to have a look and, realizing it was about the right size and probably could be bought pretty cheaply, returned to the car to urge his boss to take a look. Wally limped over to the building, agreed it was just about perfect, and decided to buy it. Just like that. It was late afternoon and there were no hotels nearby, so the two men slept in the Suburban that night.

When they woke up early the next day, they went to see the attorney who represented the building's owner. They reached an agreement after some dickering, but Wally didn't have any money with him to bind the deal. Instead, he promised to return some weeks later to complete the sale. The attorney didn't know whether to believe him or not, and was surprised when Wally returned with the promised payment some weeks later.

Once he'd acquired the building, Wally assigned Charles the job of turning it into an Airstream production plant. The place had been abandoned for years, which meant that it had to be cleaned up before any new equipment could be put into operation in the building. Charles had to hire a work force to get the plant operational.

Top: An aerial view of the new Airstream factory in Jackson Center. Erected in the 1940s as a bazooka plant, it operated during wartime and was then shuttered until Wally purchased it and had it converted to trailer production. Judging by the cars, this photo was taken around 1955. The plant is still running, producing Airstream Interstate motor coaches.

Top inset: Another scene of Jackson Center, circa 1953. A company car pulls a train loaded with trailers for delivery to waiting dealers. Airstream's advanced lightweight construction made the products easier to tow than conventional travel trailers.

Bottom inset: A typical Airstream interior from 1953. This example shows the furniture arranged as in a conventional home, though everything was fastened to the floor to keep it from moving during travel. The table with lamp affords a nice homey touch.

Jackson Center is a nice little town, neat as a pin, with small, well-kept houses and a few small commercial establishments. That said, the place is tucked away in a part of Ohio that is thinly populated, so Charles had to advertise throughout the region to find the workers he needed, mostly farm hands, laid-off machinists, and young people looking for their first jobs.

Once he had his work force, the real work began. Charles had to do everything: locate local suppliers for raw materials; find component suppliers for the toilets, sinks, ovens, and other parts he would need; arrange for power, lights, and water to the plant; and train a work force and teach them the fundamentals of building a complex product like the Airstream. Some of his workers had to be taught how to pop-rivet, some had to know woodworking, others had to be electricians, plumbers, welders, assemblers. The task was daunting.

Charles tried to hire people with the requisite skills. When he couldn't, he had to train them himself. He also had to arrange for the delivery and installation of all the tools, jigs, and fixtures needed to make his Airstream trailers. It seemed like a good idea to sign up some additional dealers to handle selling the output of the plant,

which would be in excess of what the Los Angeles plant was producing. At times, the list of problems seemed endless. But Charles was the right man for the job, and the new plant and workforce slowly came together.

In August 1952, the first Ohio-built Airstream trailer rolled out the door of the new plant. It took the small, inexperienced workforce an entire week to complete the second trailer. On a visit to the new plant, Wally was convinced that the facility could be much more productive. He promised workers a five-cent-an-hour raise if they could produce two trailers per week on a regular basis. In the third week, they did. Production continued to grow as the workers became more familiar with their jobs and the bosses worked out the kinks in the flow of production and materials.

With Charles installed as plant manager of the Jackson Center plant, and Costello running the Los Angeles plant, the problem of their power struggle seemed to be solved—for the time being. Both men were competing to see who could be the most effective manager. Wally could now get a better idea of who would be the better man to succeed him when he finally retired. Since they were running similar enterprises, it would be a simple matter of determining the better manager: product quality, cost control, and labor relations would all be good indicators.

BUILDING A DEALER NETWORK

When Airstream was first taking off, Wally thought he could limit his retail activities to selling trailers directly to customers rather than through a dealer network. This would save customers money while retaining some of the retail markup for himself. He also felt that dealing directly with his fellow enthusiasts would ensure that his customers were getting the best buying experience along with the best service, since everything would be under his direct control. Since that time, he'd realized

Wally stands in the middle of this photo, flanked by his two trusted lieutenants, Costello (left) and Charles (right). Wally had met both men while working in the defense industry during World War II. He hired them after the war to help him revive his Airstream company.

Left: A factory ad for the 1959 Airstream Land Yacht states that "Land Yachting is the magic way to travel." The popular Land Yacht was truly the king of the road when it came to travel trailers, offering a roomy, supremely comfortable vehicle.

Right: The Airstream Plastic trailer was an idea that may have been too far ahead of its time. Wally Byam promoted it because the new material was lighter than aluminum, but it was dropped after his diehard customers rejected the idea.

that retail customers needed to be able to deal with someone closer to their homes in a place, which offered new models, vehicle service, and any parts they needed.

By 1952, Airstream had an established dealer network that was considered the best in the business, though it still lacked a nationwide reach. Naturally, representation in the eastern half of the country was sparser than on the West Coast, a reflection of the high cost of shipping from its Los Angeles factory and the resulting higher prices charged for an Airstream trailer. With the new Midwest plant coming online, however, the company could offer the eastern market a lower price for delivery of a new Airstream, so it was expected that unit sales would begin to increase sharply. The new plant was ramping up quickly, and total production of Airstream trailers would soon pass previous highs.

Charles again had the situation well in hand: he built up the eastern retail network steadily, until it was on the verge of overtaking sales in the western half of the country. One of his best devices for signing new dealers was to have them attend Airstream caravans, where they could witness firsthand the intense loyalty of the Airstream customer base. Then they would hear a pitch from Claude McFaul (of the McFaul Brothers dealership)

about the benefits of becoming an Airstream dealer. The combination usually led to the prospect signing on as an Airstream dealer.

For all the success this growth portended, the dual-plant setup didn't resolve the growing competition between Costello and Charles completely. Their rivalry continued from a distance. Each branch claimed that it produced the best Airstreams, and each plant, with its own customer service center, would denigrate the other's trailers if they were brought in for service or repairs. As is often the case, there was a small kernel of truth in these allegations, since some construction techniques varied slightly between the two plants, along with the materials and components used. Whenever a difference was noted, the shop's staff would point out the variation in quality and claim that their product was better. Before long, a competitive spirit between the two operations grew to animosity, which proved detrimental to the company's two halves.

In fact, they *were* two distinct operations. Each was a separate corporate entity, rather than functioning as separate but equal parts of the same company. Even the composition of the board of directors differed for each. Why such an unusual corporate structure should be tolerated for as long as it was remains a mystery. It may have been Wally's idea that, if one company came to grief, the other would survive; after all, he'd gone bust before, and he didn't want to go through that again. Or he may have considered the possibility of one day selling one of the companies while retaining the other.

Fortunately, Wally realized that the intercompany competition he had encouraged could become unhealthy. Before long he saw the harm to his company's name and reputation that was being done as each operation badmouthed the other's workmanship. He started to address the problem in 1956 with a worker exchange program, where workers from each plant spent time at the other plant, absorbing the culture and learning different construction techniques. In addition, management personnel from both plants were required to meet together quarterly to exchange ideas. Today such programs are common throughout most industries and are instituted to promote the use of "best practices" throughout a company's global operations. These programs ensure that the best methods from each plant are used consistently within the organization to attain the highest quality and productivity possible.

In Wally's case, he wanted to, as he put it, "develop the spirit of 'one Airstream.'" Years later, the salvation of Ford Motor Company would come when new CEO Alan Mulally instituted his "One Ford" concept, an idea similar to what Wally instituted in the 1950s.

Having survived this internal turmoil, Airstream Trailers continued to grow. While he was in charge, there was no time for a divisive atmosphere to tear down all that Wally had worked so hard to create.

THE FABULOUS FIFTIES

For America and its citizens, the 1950s was one of the most exciting and promising decades of all time, in part because of the flood of innovative products that came into common use with the adoption of televisions, jet airplanes, and flashy automobiles loaded with new options and futuristic styling. It was a decade of innovation and advances—and Airstream wasn't about to be left behind.

Under Wally's direction, Airstream engineers came out with a continuous stream of new ideas for trailer designs. One of the better ones, a fiberglass-bodied travel trailer dubbed the Airstream Plastic Trailer, didn't catch on with Airstream loyalists; hardcore aluminum devotees (also known as rivetheads) simply weren't interested in anything else. In addition, the cost of building a trailer out of fiberglass was considerably more than producing an aluminum job, and the resulting higher price tag made the plastic models harder to sell.

Another idea sounded good at first: brightly colored trailers that mimicked the tones of flashy 1950s cars. These variations didn't catch on, either. After much experimentation, the idea was abandoned.

Wally and Stella had the Airstream plant create a special gold-anodized trailer for themselves, but the attractive finish didn't hold up, oxidizing to a dull sheen. The trailer still exists, part of the factory's collection of historic Airstreams.

Another innovation, the Wally Byam Holiday trailer, was an inexpensive, basic 15-footer with a riveted aluminum skin. Too many compromises had been made in the name of cutting costs, though, and customers complained that the Holiday looked more like a canned ham than an Airstream product. One of Airstream's few failed production models, it was dropped after fewer than 100 were produced.

For all these design misses, the 1950s were a golden decade for Airstream, as the company grew in leaps and bounds. One area of growth came in purchasing companies within the supply chain, which helped to streamline operations and reduce overall production costs.

Always looking for ways to expand his operations, Charles developed a plan to acquire two of his suppliers. The first, Leininger Brothers, was a lumberyard and manufacturer headquartered in Jackson Center that produced the cabinets that went

Top: Construction of the body shell for a new trailer in 1955, probably in the Jackson Center plant. A lot of handwork went into the construction of an Airstream, a hallmark of trailer production that continues to this day.

Bottom left: Installing the vehicle's wiring systems. The man wearing a tie on the right is probably a quality control manager.

Bottom right: A young lady rivets overhead cabinets into place. Using rivets, while more expensive than using nails or screws, provides a much better hold than other fasteners.

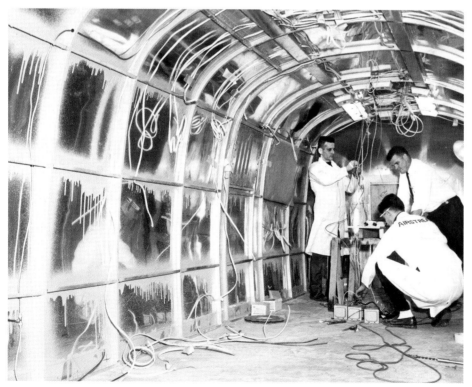

The Airstream frame featured a very low floor height and stout construction. The monocoque body shell added to this base created a lightweight but extremely sturdy vehicle that was easier to tow than those produced by competitors.

into Airstreams. Charles also had his eye on the Henchen Company, which built Airstream's axles. After showing Wally cost charts illustrating how much the company would save from these purchases, Charles got the go-ahead to acquire both firms. Charles also asked for and received funding to double the manufacturing space at the Jackson Center assembly building. He was growing sales at a steady pace and needed more vehicles.

The rival Los Angeles operation was not to be outdone while the Ohio plant expanded and achieved additional production output. When demand began to outstrip production capacity, Costello petitioned Wally for permission to expand his manufacturing footprint. In 1956, he was given the green light to build a second plant at 12804 East Firestone Boulevard in nearby Norwalk, California.

With his companies running well, sales going strong, and growth assured for the foreseeable future, Wally decided to spend more time on other aspects of the Airstream brand. He set out on more caravans than ever

before, motivated by a simple desire to see the world. He traveled to Denmark in 1953 to visit the International Trailer Rally, a trailer meet-and-show that included product displays from most of the major European trailer manufacturers. Here he was able to pick up new ideas for interior styling and layouts as well as mechanical innovations. Some of these began to show up in the 1954 Airstream products, including the "Safari," which featured a dinette located at the front of the trailer and a kitchen at the side. These variations increased the area available for windows, greatly improving the amount of natural light inside the trailer and giving interior a brighter, airier feel.

Many of Wally's customers had shared their desire for a hot water heating system. He took the problem to heart and managed to convince Mark Bowen of the Bowen Water Heater Company to create the first such system to be installed in a trailer, which was quickly added to his products. As always, Airstream led the way in product innovation.

In 1955, Wally led the largest caravan ever—totaling 500 trailers—to western Mexico, a sight that must have boggled the minds of other travelers on the road. The trip went well, having been carefully planned in advance. This was a great year for Airstream, though Wally's own health problems came to the fore when he suffered a heart attack. He'd been working too hard and, in all likelihood, playing too hard as well.

In the same year, a new organization related to Airstream was founded. On a caravan to Nova Scotia that included nearly 100 trailers, owners decided to found a new club dedicated to the Airstream lifestyle. In honor of the man they revered for pioneering that lifestyle, they chose to name the new club the Wally Byam Caravan Club (WBCC). When word got out to other Airstream enthusiasts about the new club, membership skyrocketed.

CARAVANNING TO EUROPE

The 1956 model year saw Airstream introduce its new Overlander International trailer, with a fashionable interior divided into three main areas—a spacious living room and galley up front, roomy bedroom in the middle (with choice of a double bed or twins), and a bathroom at the rear. It was a good vehicle (and a good name) and one that reflected Wally's interest in taking Airstream even further afield. His confidence in his product was unbounded. Since he'd begun scouting out caravan routes well in advance of the actual journey, Wally was completely confident that a relatively anxiety-free trip was possible, even when it involved a long journey with dozens of participants.

After taking in the latest from Airstream's European competitors at the 1955 International Trailer rally in France, Wally ranged around the continent scouting the route for a six-month European caravanning excursion. Scouting for Wally was an intensive, detail-oriented activity: he visited potential camping areas, checked border and customs regulations, arranged for receptions by the locals en route, measured the heights of underpasses, and even recorded weather forecasts. He used this data to map out a comprehensive itinerary.

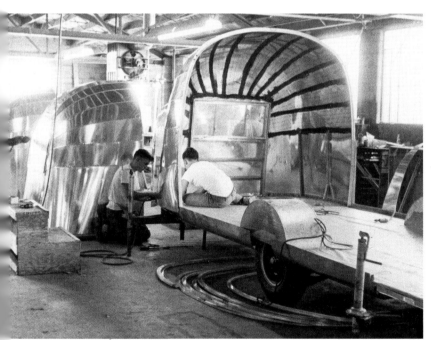 

Left: The endcaps of an Airstream vehicle were always the most time-consuming and expensive parts to produce. They were made of a series of mildly rounded panels riveted to stout ribs, along with lower walls and windows that were fitted into place.

Right: Two men carry a nearly completed Airstream shell in 1955. Note the many small pieces of aluminum used to form a curvature on the end piece.

Top: A large Airstream trailer during construction, 1955. The shell has been attached to the frame; now it's time to begin window installation.

Bottom: Another factory scene, also from 1955. The building appears to be the Jackson Center plant. In this photo, the trailers are nearly complete, with only some finish work needed on the interiors. Soon they'll be ready to ship to dealers.

With his usual tongue-in-cheek humor, Wally wrote a word of advice for obtaining an International Driver's License: "Have six horrible-looking passport-type photos made of each person who is going to drive your car," he wrote. He also provided information on which vaccinations were needed for travel, as well as information on car insurance and vehicle shipping costs. As he well knew, it would take extensive planning, lots of effort from unpaid volunteers, and a little bit of luck as well.

In April 1956, the European caravan assembled in Rotterdam, Holland, with thirty-eight cars towing trailers. The Dutch greeted the members of the excursion warmly, with flowers for each lady traveler, mugs for the men, and candy, fruit, and cheeses for all. Before setting off, cars were tuned and serviced, and trailers gone over, with brakes, shocks, and tires checked on all vehicles. Leaving Rotterdam, the caravan slowly wound its way toward Belgium. The following day they parked in Breda

A 1950s family stops to photograph some Seminole Indians in Florida, circa 1955.

Top: Wally Byam was a good showman with a great sense of humor. Here he combines both traits by showing off two Airstream trailers: the larger "Nursery" and the smaller "Mother-in-Law" apartment. Note the signs in the windows indicating some of the best features of the sturdy Airstreams.

Left: In this November 1955 photo, Wally helps cook some steaks for that year's Airstream Trailer Rally and Family Reunion. Some 350 customers attended the gala event in Palm Springs, California.

and were greeted with calliope music accompanying a troupe of dancing children, while the locals plied them with coffee, hot chocolate, and more candy. When they departed Breda the next day, they were saluted with loud factory whistles and clanging church bells. In Brussels, they were greeted heartily by the US ambassador to Belgium, the Honorable Frederick M. Alger.

At each stop, the travelers were treated like royalty and welcomed by the local residents. When they arrived at the Lille Fair in France, motorcycle policemen escorted the caravan with "The Star-Spangled Banner" playing on their loudspeakers. The minister of agriculture planted dramatic kisses on Wally's cheeks as he welcomed the group to his country.

Paris offered its always exciting spectacles and attractions, and the group remained for several weeks, sampling its extraordinary restaurants, shops, and sights. They parked in the Bois de Boulogne, a beautiful 2,090-acre park located along the western edge of the city's 16th arrondissement that entranced the visiting Airstreamers with its calm serenity and vast beauty.

The caravan served as a self-contained, miniature village as they proceeded. The travelers even set up their own government, an uncomplicated one-man/one-vote system. They got together to vote on various issues, including how far and how fast to travel on each leg of the journey and on what days they would travel. Each problem was voted on and resolved to everyone's satisfaction. An official "caboose" was designated for those who lagged behind on the trip, with a driver bringing up the rear to make sure no one was left behind because of vehicle problems, breakdowns, or losing their way. Wally relinquished the role of "Wagonmaster" for the trip, letting someone else scout out the next campsite, though Wally had already done much of the preliminary planning. Others were in charge of mail delivery, rushing out to local post offices to pick up any mail that had been forwarded there.

Wally was in his element, showing off at various stops by dressing in his customary odd outfits (buckskin shirt, jeans, and his ever-present blue beret), calling meetings to order with a circus barker's cry of "Hurry, Hurry, Hurry! Come one, come all! It's meeting time!"

Left: A red 1955 Buick stands ready to hook up to this vintage Airstream and head off for adventure. Note the jalousie windows in the door.
Right: The big Buick, now hooked up and ready to take off on an adventure.

While in Paris, the Arc de Triomphe is a must-see landmark, as this western-garbed couple can attest. Begun in 1806 by order of Napoleon, the monument was created to honor his Grande Armée's victories.

In interviews with journalists along the way, Wally altered his life story, casting Stella as the partner who had first complained about sleeping on the ground, and who had traveled with him in his "platform tent," from which he derived his innovative trailer design. He also mentioned working at Lockheed during the war, speaking as if he had created the original aluminum Airstream based on Lockheed's use of the material. Perhaps he did all this creative re-telling to simplify the story for the press, or maybe he wanted to spare Stella any embarrassing questions.

In Reims, the group toured the Pommery and Greno estate, home to probably the greatest purveyor of champagne in the world. Members were invited to tour the underground labyrinth where the champagne is stored in an 11½-mile network of tunnels connecting 120 quarries. There they saw some of the more than twelve *million* bottles of wine stored in racks that line the tunnels. The temperature within the underground vaults is a steady 50 degrees year round, perfect for aging wines.

The caravan also stopped to visit the great military cemeteries at Belleau Wood, Chateau Thierry, and

Verdun, the site of many soldier burials from World War I. Cruising through Luxembourg, they also stopped to visit the grave of Gen. George S. Patton, commander of the US Third Army and hero of the World War II.

Perhaps not surprisingly, the tour group picked up some new members along the way. An American couple on vacation was so impressed by the line of trailers that they decided to buy an English model and join the group on the spot. At another stop, a guest from the George V Hotel, one of the finest hotels in France, decided to quit the hotel immediately to join the caravan; he purchased a VW Microbus with a camper conversion and became the newest caravan member.

As they moved on to Germany, the caravaners impressed the locals with the "Prussian Efficiency" employed to set up camp each night. The usual objective was to arrange the trailers in a wagon-wheel formation. The secret of their precision lay in the behind-the-scenes efforts of the Wagonmaster—he and some volunteers marked out the spaces in advance and guided each trailer into position.

Then it was on to Dusseldorf, Germany, where they settled in for the night in a park by the Rhine River. Cruising the Autobahn, they moved on to Frankfurt and then to Heidelberg, where they camped alongside the lovely Neckar River. After several more stops, they crossed into Switzerland, with its beautiful postcard mountains, green meadows, and smiling, friendly people.

By the time they crossed the Alps into Austria, it was early June. Nevertheless, they ran into heavy snow that halted their journey for a night. But the next day they were able to navigate the foot-deep snow, reach the summit, and head down the mountains into Innsbruck, camping just outside that ancient city.

The next stop on their journey was Italy, where the travelers enjoyed the beauty of Trieste, Venice, Florence,

PALM SPRINGS AIRSTREAM RALLY, 1958

Above: Why walk around the campsite when you can ride a scooter? Bringing a scooter to Europe also made it easier for many people to navigate the crowded European streets while sightseeing.

Right: Wally Byam helps a fellow traveler. Traveling in a caravan was much better than traveling alone, because there were always people around to help navigate.

A trailer hooked up to a 1955 Chrysler, probably indicating the year this photo was taken. The setting is a pyramid in Mexico, probably Chichen Itza. The Airstream owners can enjoy this setting, with no crowds of tourists.

and the Italian Riviera. Then it was on to the glories of Rome, the Vatican City, the everlastingly beautiful St. Peter's Square, the fabled seven hills, and the Coliseum. They continued on to Naples, Pompeii, Sorrento, and Capri.

The entire trip took six months. By the end, the caravaners had traveled through sixteen countries. The travelers returned to the United States a bit tired, a little homesick, and profoundly changed by their experiences. It had truly been the trip of a lifetime.

With the exception of the Cuba caravan, this was Wally's first attempt at shepherding a large caravan on a trip across the ocean, followed by a long land journey. After it was over, the trip was written up in a major article that appeared in the June 1957 issue of *National Geographic*, a major coup for Airstream. Written

by Norma Miller with accompanying photography by her husband Ardean Miller, the article relates all the fun and adventures to be had in a life on the road in an engrossing, compelling fashion.

AIRSTREAM'S CHANGING OF THE GUARD

During 1957, after twenty-seven years building Airstream trailers, Wally was finally ready to hand Airstream over to someone else. The business remained in two halves, though, with Charles serving as president of Airstream Trailers, Inc. of Ohio, while Costello became president of Airstream Trailers, Inc. of California.

Though industry sales topped $600 million in 1955, the outlook was uncertain for the travel trailer market. The year of the European caravan trip had seen a slight slowing in business activity; by August 1957, the US economy had slipped into a recession as interest rates climbed and consumers cut back on major purchases. The automotive and housing industries were hit particularly hard, with sales tumbling badly.

Wally instructed his two presidents to seek new ways to cut costs, lest they slip into bad habits that would endanger his beloved Airstream. "It will take BLOOD, SWEAT, TEARS, . . . and GUTS! . . . to keep Airstream alive in the next six months," he warned them. He advised them to look at every nickel four times before spending it, negotiate on every price quoted, and cut inventory levels and work in progress to the bare minimum. And he cautioned them to have the courage to raise prices when necessary. "Eternal vigilance is the price of success," he told them. "In tough times it is doubly so."

Top right: This Airstream, circa 1955, features an attractive side window treatment that provides lots of light to the interior for a bright, airy feeling.

Bottom: A display of Airstream trailers at a sports complex, probably the site of a trailer show. Note the vehicle on the left with GB (for Great Britain) tags and markings, indicating it's the "World's Most Traveled Trailer."

During the late 1950s, Wally came up with the idea of offering painted Airstream trailers. The colors were to be as loud and bright as 1950s automobiles. The factory produced several, including this special gold anodized trailer owned by Wally and Stella Byam. Unfortunately, the paint technology of the day meant that the paints quickly faded, becoming unsightly. This vehicle has been completely restored by the factory, with the colors returned to their original luster. The building in the left background is the Airstream Customer Service building in Jackson Center.

In 1958, Airstream introduced an innovative idea to help support its customers when they traveled on company-sponsored caravans. Called the Byam Bath, it was an all-white, 26-foot Airstream trailer fitted with showers and electrical outlets so that any camper who didn't have a proper shower in his trailer could use the Byam Bath. Users could plug their electric razors into the outlets to get a shave as well. A new trailer also debuted in 1958, the fittingly named Sovereign of the Road, with a commodious interior and four trailer wheels for better balance and easier towing.

Wally and Stella hit the road again that year, traveling to Central America with a caravan of Airstream trailers as well as the now-famous Byam Bath trailer. This trip was filmed and shown on the ABC television network under the title *South to Costa Rica*. An earlier caravan— the 1956 journey to Mexico—had also been filmed and televised by ABC, broadcast as *The Silver Caravan* because every trailer featured was an Airstream.

It was during 1958 that the Wally Byam Caravan Club planned its first International Rally, modeled along the lines of the European Rallies that Wally and a number

Left: Wally and Stella in 1956, with one of their trailers. This one also appears to be painted, though the color cannot be determined from this image. The bicycle seen here has a small gasoline engine; Wally used this bike on caravans to zoom around large campsites, keeping in touch with all the members. He also used a scooter at times.

Top: The factory reconditioning of the Byam gold trailer extended even to replicating the original names painted on the side by the door.

Stella and Wally lift the key to the city of "Byamville." For Wally Byam's sixty-second birthday on July 4, 1958, members of the Wally Byam Caravan Club decided to hold their first annual rally in Bull Shoals, Arkansas, which they renamed Byamville in his honor. Since that time it has become a tradition to hold a rally on Wally's birthday.

AIRSTREAM HOLIDAY

of his customers had attended. The Club chose Bull Shoals, Arkansas, for the meet, and decided it was high time to include a special tribute to Wally, the man who had done more than anyone else to create the Airstream lifestyle. They decided the Rally would be an ideal place to celebrate his sixty-second birthday. They did a few whimsical things, like renaming Bull Shoals "Byamville" (a big improvement, in retrospect), and dubbing a local street "Byam Boulevard." The meet was a huge success, spawning a tradition that lives to this day: every year on the Fourth of July, the Wally Byam Caravan Club holds its International Rally somewhere in North America. The date honors Wally, keeping alive the memory of his work, his innovations, and his undying sense of adventure.

Under the direction of Airstream's new presidents, advertising was ramped up. A six-figure budget funded ads in a wide variety of publications, including *True Travel*,

Airstream ads were sometimes wistful, sometimes clever, but they were always entertaining. Who could argue with the statement: "It's Time to Enjoy Life?" The car in the front of the line is a 1957 Ford.

IT'S TIME TO ENJOY LIFE

"Come, fill the cup, and in the fire of Spring your Winter garment of repentance fling: The bird of time has but a little way to flutter and the bird is on the wing..."

Heed the Poet's advice: Hitch up your Airstream and be off on the highroad of travel-adventure, with old Winter at your back and the wondrous beauties of this broad land ahead. An Airstream featherweight travel trailer is your answer to Spring's siren call...go where you like, stay as long as you please in unmatched luxurious comfort. No clocks, calendars or timetables to restrict your motion; no reservations, baggage or inferior accommodations to dampen your enthusiasm. Airstream provides complete self-containment in a sleek, easy-to-tow package: lights, water, refrigeration, bathroom facilities, comfortable beds and the neatest shipshape galley you ever cooked in. Travel tested on the roads of the world, Airstream is guaranteed for life...the good life, the life you should be leading right now. See your Airstream dealer today!

JOIN ONE OF WALLY BYAM'S EXCITING AIRSTREAM CARAVANS

 AIRSTREAM TRAILERS, INC.

GO AIRSTREAM

Write for interesting free literature and see your Airstream dealer.

write nearest factory: 107 CHURCH ST., JACKSON CENTER, OHIO • 12804 E. FIRESTONE BLVD., NORWALK, CALIF.

ADVENTURE IS YOUR COMPANION IN AN AIRSTREAM!

Wherever you venture . . . via the twinkling Paris boulevards . . . the inviting beaches splashed with color and laughter along the sunny Riviera . . . and through every friendly little picturesque village along the way . . . fun and high spirits ride with you. Excitement seems to dash ahead in order to join you at your next unscheduled stop. As commander of your own Land Yacht, your mood is your only itinerary. You'll never think of reservations or hotel prices. Just glance in your rear view mirror to remind yourself that your handsome craft is following with every comfort: Comfortable beds, heat, lights, hot and cold running water, a complete bathroom . . . all independent of outside sources. Inspect the completely self-contained Land Yacht at your Airstream dealer right away. Then go . . . do . . . live! Don't delay, for life is a one-time thing . . . enjoy it!

Left: Talk about lucky people: this couple touring France own a beautiful 1957 Airstream *and* a 1957 Cadillac. Even back then, Airstream owners tended to travel more often than owners of other travel trailers, and to more far-flung destinations.

Bottom: A family stops to take pictures and converse with a Native American in Manitou Springs, Colorado. The American West was an especially popular destination for vacationers in the late 1950s and early 1960s.

Right: A couple in their new Airstream with a 1958 Ford. One of the best things about traveling by trailer is that you get to see beautiful scenery, and you can stop anytime you wish.

Bottom: Unlabeled photo from the Airstream company archives. The car is a circa 1959 Desoto, while the foliage looks southern. Florida, perhaps?

Top: Wally hosted a big get-together to interest people in his most ambitious caravan to date—a journey through Africa that was planned for 1959. The large gorilla statue was pure Wally-style showmanship, as were the pith helmets worn for the occasion.

Left: Wally scouts the route ahead, or maybe he's just enjoying a good view. Cowboy boots were a favorite part of his attire.

National Geographic, *Scientific American*, *Fifty Plus*, and *Sports Illustrated*. The company made sure to keep its name in the newspapers as well, regularly sending out press releases detailing the exciting exploits of Airstream owners and their trailers.

An Airstream trailer was even one of the "stars" of a short-lived weekly television series that appeared in 1959–1960. Called *Troubleshooters*, the show featured the adventures of a globetrotting construction crew, with the Airstream serving as their on-the-road headquarters. Running for thirty-nine action-packed episodes, the series starred the ever-popular actor Keenan Wynn and Olympian athlete Bob Mathias. Most of the episodes were directed by a then-unknown Robert Altman, although one episode was directed by actor Paul Henreid of *Casablanca* fame.

America was on a building spree in the 1950s, constructing the national road system dubbed the Dwight D. Eisenhower National System of Interstate and Defense Highways, more commonly known as the Interstate Highway System. President Eisenhower had championed its formation as a necessary and long-overdue defense measure. He had realized years earlier that part of Germany's success in the opening days of World War II had come about because of its superior highway system, the Autobahn, which made rushing troops, equipment, and supplies from point to point quick and efficient. The Autobahn had also helped Germany defend its home turf in the closing days of the war. Eisenhower was able to argue convincingly that America also needed a national road network that could speed men and materials anywhere across the country in the event of an emergency. Construction was authorized by the Federal Aid Highway Act of 1956 and paving began on September 26 of that year. As of 2013, the Interstate Highway System has a total length of 47,856 miles.

WALLY'S CARAVANS

1951-52 - Mexico & Central America
1952-53 - Mexico West Coast
1954 - Mexico East Coast
1954 - Western Canada
1955 - Mexico West Coast
1955 - Eastern Canada
1955 - Mexico
1956 - Europe
1956 - Cuba
1957 - Mexico
1957 - Kentucky Derby & Indianapolis 500
1958 - Oregon Trail
1958 - Cuba
1958 - Mexico
1958 - Central America
1958 - Western Canada
1959 - Mexico
1959-60 - Africa, Near East, Europe

Above: At the very beginning of the African Caravan, Wally greets fellow caravaner Grace Ziegler on their arrival in Cape Town, South Africa. Thousands of miles of adventure still lay ahead of the hardy band of travelers.

Opposite top: Wally and Stella in October 1959 speaking with native Pygmies in the Belgian Congo, a scene later used in Airstream print advertisements. Wally has placed his pith helmet on one of the men as a well-dressed Stella looks on from the doorway.

Opposite, left inset: Look closely at this photo and you can see the long line of Airstream trailers stretched out behind the lead vehicles. This photo was taken somewhere in southern Ethiopia. During the trip, Wally was introduced to Emperor Haile Selassie I, whose titles, in addition to Emperor of Ethiopia, included Elect of God, Conquering Lion of the Tribe of Judah, King of Zion, and King of Kings.

Opposite, right inset: A print ad employing the "Pygmy" photo.

Somewhere in southern Ethiopia

ETHIOPIA...
at their Airstream doorsteps!

Over incredibly primitive roads and camel trails, in virtually the same condition as when they were built, over 1,500 years B.C.; up into the mountain fastnesses of an African kingdom that was ancient when the Romans invaded Britain; through a region cut off from the world by immense distance and by sheer altitude, this Wally Byam Caravan of silver Airstreams is seen threading its way through Ethiopia.

Every Airstream in this Friendly Task Force of Good Will is as sound and roadworthy as on the day it proudly swung into line on the great trek up the vast continent of Africa from Capetown to Cairo; every owner is enjoying familiar American comforts, conveniences, and luxuries, from ice cubes to tubs and showers — from switch-on lights to sprawl-out beds.

Africa-Caravan ruggedness, light weight, fleetness, and total self-containment is built-in with *every* Land Yacht, including the models you can inspect at your Airstream Dealer. Drive over and see them today.

Wally Byam with Haile Selassie I, Elect of God, Conquering Lion of the Tribe of Judah, King of Zion, King of Kings, Emperor of Ethiopia

Wally & Stella Byam with their Airstream Land Yacht among the Pygmies of the Belgian Congo. Oct. 1959

YOU CAN BE THERE...
IN A LAND YACHT

Probably you will never want to visit with the Batwa Tribe of Pygmies in the Belgian Congo; nor would you plan to thread your way overland from Capetown, South Africa, to Oslo, Norway, as 41 happy-go-Airstream families in 41 sturdy Land Yachts* are doing right now. The important point is — *you could if you wanted to!*

These 41 representative American families are enjoying every accustomed convenience and comfort — showers, tubs, city-type electric lighting, latest model refrigerators and gas ovens, rich decor, and wonderful stretch-out beds every night everywhere, whether they find themselves in the lion country of Kenya or navigating the great Nubian Desert by compass.

No matter where *you* plan to go — and stay; no matter how far away and how remote — to a coral decorated Key in Florida, or on a palm-ornamented strand near Acapulco, your Airstream will eagerly and delightfully serve you — with stay-at-home surroundings, appliances, and luxuries, always awaiting your pleasure, five steps and five seconds away. Yes, you can be there in a Land Yacht, and your friendly Airstream Dealer is waiting to show you how. Drive over and see him Today.

Only Airstream construction will take you anywhere in the world. Write for free literature and nearest dealer.

"IF IT ISN'T AN AIRSTREAM, IT ISN'T A LAND YACHT."

WALLY BYAM **AIRSTREAM** INC.

Wally Byam's Caravan through AFRICA

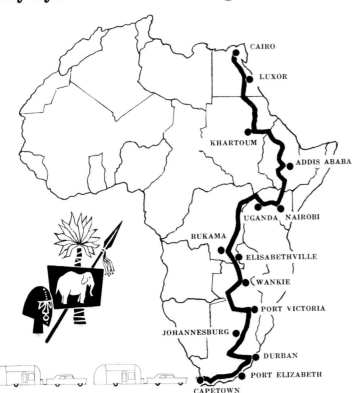

The planned route of the 1959 Caravan through Africa, which began in Cape Town, South Africa, and wound its way north to Cairo, Egypt.

Top: Looking like an African safari leader, Wally Byam poses for this photo at the start of the African Caravan. His vehicle is a 1957 International four-door pickup with a special body on the back, towing one of his several Airstream trailers. Wally and Stella tended to prefer smaller Airstream trailers, even for long-distance travel. Wally's favorite tow vehicle was the rugged International; he owned several different models over the years.

Above: On the road in Ethiopia, this traveler's International truck with a handy camper cap on the back got stuck in the mud. Thankfully, he has plenty of men to help push him out of the muck. Judging by the beret and cowboy boots, that's Wally Byam looking on.

One result of all the road construction was an explosive increase in American road travel. With thousands of miles of bright new highways beckoning them, millions of hit the road, taking to heart Dinah Shore's admonition to "See the USA." Although Dinah suggested doing so in a Chevrolet, thousands of savvy travelers saw the country in an Airstream trailer.

This new demand resulted in a sharp sales increase for both Airstream companies. By the end of the decade, the businesses had the combined capacity to build up to fifty-five trailers a week—and still the plants couldn't keep up with demand.

Airstream was known around the world. Wally was enjoying all the hard-won prosperity and recognition, but he wasn't sitting in a rocking chair reminiscing. While his company prospered, he continued taking part in his beloved caravans, teaching newcomers the ropes, and bringing experienced travelers to new destinations. He seemed to have limitless energy, enjoying every moment on the road.

For 1959, Wally decided it was time to attempt the greatest caravan of all time. Now in his sixties, he hatched a plan to lead a group of intrepid travelers on a true adventure of a lifetime: a trip from Cape Town, South Africa, to Cairo, Egypt, across some of the most difficult terrain on the planet. It was bold, daring, and more than a little dangerous. Wally had no trouble finding others willing to try. Sure, it would be strenuous, he told them, but it would also be fun. And so it was—one of the most daring and audacious trips ever, a true tribute to Wally's vision.

Airstream was riding high in 1959. The brand's popularity reached an all-time high, and sales catapulted off the charts. The futurist Buckminster Fuller, father of the famed geodesic dome, taught classes in an Airstream, while thousands of Americans vacationed in their own personal "Fifth Avenue on Wheels," as Wally liked to call his Airstreams. Wally, Stella, and all the men and women toiling away at Airstream looked to the future with renewed confidence.

Above: Another International truck towing an Airstream on the caravan through Africa, this time stopping among the Avenue of the Sphinxes in Egypt. The African Caravan was one of the most exciting and exotic of the caravans that Wally led.

Below: Another stop along the route in Africa, here visiting some ancient ruins.

Right: Lucky Airstream caravaners got to visit the original Abu Simbel site during the African Caravan. This fabulous monument, located in Nubia, Southern Egypt, was moved to a new location during the 1960s to make way for the much-needed Aswan Dam.

Below: A couple of International pickups tow their trailers across a small, sturdy-looking bridge spanning a deep gorge in Africa.

Top: On the road in Africa, location unknown. Note the two men in the left foreground carrying rifles for protection from lions and tigers.

Below left: The entire caravan group inspects Egyptian monuments in 1959. Note the large number of berets. Wally Byam began wearing a blue beret on an earlier trip to France and liked it so much he wore it on many subsequent trips. It eventually became a sort of trademark among Airstream enthusiasts and remains a popular accessory to this day.

Below right: Iowa natives Arthur and Ellen Martin are pictured standing by fabulous Victoria Falls in southern Africa on the Zambezi River, at the border of Zambia and Zimbabwe.

Top: Lined up in front of the former bazooka plant in Jackson Center are the many Airstream employees in 1960. This building is still in use as a production plant for Airstream's luxurious Interstate motor coaches.

Opposite page: Where you been? For Airstream owners, that's no idle question. The owner of this trailer has been to Indiana, Ohio, New York (including Niagara Falls), Montana, Massachusetts, Flroida, Minnesota, Lousiana, and many other states. Airstream owners are travelers.

CHAPTER FOUR

DAYS OF GLORY: 1960–1973

Airstream kept busy at the dawn of the 1960s. The new Interstate Highway System encouraged millions of Americans to take to the road, traveling to beaches, mountains, national parks, resorts, and historic sites. While such journeys fired their imaginations, many didn't relish having to search for a hotel room at each stop along the way; they also recognized that bringing accommodations along with them would be a great cost saver.

Right: This scene appears to be in Switzerland, though it could be elsewhere. The time? About 1960, judging by the 1960 Ford station wagon pulling the trailer.

Bottom: This postcard scene shows a caravan of Airstream trailers, most likely the group that started out in 1959, arrayed in the classic Airstream "wagon-wheel" encampment next to the Great Pyramid at El Gizeh in Egypt.

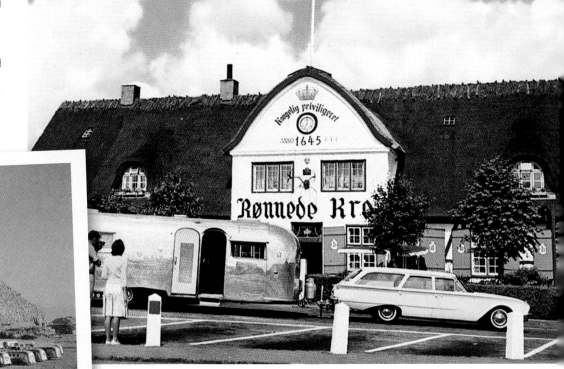

THE GREAT PYRAMID AT EL GIZEH, EGYPT, 1960

This was a contributing factor for the company's success in this period, as orders for new Airstream trailers poured into its two factories. From a total production level of fifty-five trailers a week in 1961, output soared to eighty-five trailers per week by 1962—50 units from the burgeoning Ohio plant and 35 from the Los Angeles facility. Even with this huge increase, though, the company was barely able to keep up with demand.

THE TORCH IS PASSED

Now in semiretirement, Wally was no longer involved in day-to-day operations, though he still kept watch over his life's work. Living in their comfortable hilltop bungalow at 3684 Roseview Avenue in Los Angeles's Mount Washington section, he and Stella enjoyed their shared interests. Wally's home was a reflection of the man

himself—compact, solid, comfortable, and unassuming. It was modest but interesting. In this little castle they could entertain their many visitors; if anyone wanted to stay over for a few days, the couple had three Airstream trailers parked in the yard, ready to serve as guest homes.

These were quiet, reflective times for Wally, moments to enjoy the fruits of his labor. He could look back on all the good he'd accomplished in his life and feel proud of himself. "We feel that we have spread more honest-to-goodness, down-to-earth goodwill in the countries we've visited than all the striped-pants ambassadors put together," he said, and he was right: Wally and his fellow caravaners had met and mingled with the people of the countries they visited, rather than simply the politicos. He and his friends had lived among the people, not in hotels or embassies.

Beginning in the 1950s, Harry Halbritter and his wife Allene, of San Diego, California, declared themselves the "World's Travelingest Caravaners." They could prove it simply by pointing to the many trips they'd taken, which were listed on the side of their Airstream trailer.

Right: This ad, from 1960, advertises the trip itself rather than the product. It was to be quite a journey, traveling through France, Holland, Austria, Belgium, and Italy. Who wouldn't have wanted to go?

Bottom: The Atomium in Heysel Park in Brussels, about 1960. This structure was originally built for the 1958 Brussels World's Fair. Designed by engineer André Waterkeyn and architects André and Jean Polak, it is 335 feet tall, with nine stainless-steel spheres, each 59 feet in diameter, connected to form the shape of a molecule of iron crystal magnified 165 billion times. It stands today as part of a museum.

The good times wouldn't last, though. In 1960, Wally was diagnosed with brain cancer. Treatment involved a grueling series of operations, all unsuccessful. Although Wally remained cheerfully combative, fighting cancer with his characteristic determination, in the end he succumbed to the illness. He died just eighteen days after his sixty-sixth birthday on July 22, 1962. His ashes were interred at Forest Lawn Cemetery, the final resting place of many Hollywood celebrities and movie stars. Now he was with the same crowd he had yearned to join when he first came to California.

Ever since he could remember, Wally had longed to be famous. By the time of his death, he had achieved that goal, known as he was across the country as a true pioneer in travel trailers, the visionary and talented owner of the most famous brand of trailers in the world. For a kid from a small town in Oregon, he'd done all right.

Wally's death affected many people. Naturally, his legions of friends and all his fellow caravan travelers were greatly saddened by his passing. But there was trouble at the two Airstream companies. During their years as the heads of their respective halves of the Airstream empire, Costello and Charles had bided their

The Acapulco Naval Base, where a large group of Airstream enthusuasts stopped for a visit. As the 1960s progressed, the number of caravan trips increased.

Top: Immediately after Wally's death, the company remained as two separate entities. When the California and Ohio branches merged into one company in late 1963, Art Costello was named president of the company, only the second president in more than thirty years.

Left: The International Travelall was always a favorite of Airstream veterans because it was large and powerful, capable of pulling an Airstream effortlessly. In addition, the Travelall could carry as many as eight passengers and hold a huge amount of cargo. Cleared out, the back area could even be used as an extra bedroom, providing the rear seat was folded down.

time for just this moment. Both had drafted plans for taking over management of the company. Having made alliances with different members of the two boards of directors, both leaders moved toward a showdown, where the two companies would merge into one—with only one president in command.

In November 1962, mere months after Wally's passing, Airstream of Ohio and Airstream of California combined in a new company called Airstream, Inc. With business still booming, the new company needed both plants for manufacturing the ever-in-demand trailers. Ownership of the combined company transferred to Stella.

This didn't change the East Coast–West Coast tensions. The situation remained tense for everyone, as Charles and Costello continually tried to outdo

one another in their quest to become top executive of the company. Their constant maneuvering and one-upmanship disrupted the company's once-harmonious atmosphere. Finally, the board of directors could stand no more: in late 1963, a board meeting was called to appoint the new president of the consolidated Airstream, Inc.

The meeting took place at a hotel in Chicago (midway between the two factions' home turf, therefore "neutral territory"). Costello showed up early, accompanied by a group of his supporters as a show of force. Charles was there as well; he remained in the hallway for a few extra moments, combing his hair and mustache to perfection and readying himself to grab as much attention as possible. The directors called the meeting to order at

Top: A happy couple in Acapulco in 1960 with a fine haul of swordfish. Airstream owners tend to live more exciting and fulfilling lives than other people, with trailers that enable and encourage them to see the world.

Left: Another ad for Airstream, featuring a big 1960s Rolls-Royce, the very symbol of exclusive luxury. Joining this auto literally and figuratively with the plush Airstream Land Yacht was a smart marketing move.

8:30 a.m. sharp. It seems that they never expected to hold a frank discussion of the two men's merits, since (apparently) there had never been any doubt among them as to who would be the winner.

Within moments, someone motioned to put the choice to a vote. The votes were cast in less than a minute, and Costello was named president. Fashionably late by two minutes, Charles made his grand entrance to a meeting that was nearly over. He put on the best face possible and accepted the decision. He had lost in what seems to have

The awesome gathering for the 1962 Wally Byam Caravan Club International meet, seen from the air. The trailers are arranged in the classic Airstream "wagon wheel."

been a fixed contest, though he came away with a pretty good second prize: the directors named him Airstream, Inc.'s new chairman of the board. In a way, he was now Costello's boss, though in reality the presidency held more real power; practically speaking, Costello would be the man in charge of running the company.

The whole transition of power could have ended on a positive note, but Costello's friends had a final slap in the face they wanted to deliver to Charles. It was a specially made paperweight, featuring a clock with its hands set at 8:32. Mean-spirited and completely unnecessary, this little jab is indicative of the sort of people attracted to Costello.

Stella died in 1964, a year after the meeting, thus ending the era in which the founders of Airstream were still associated with the company. Now it was up to the new management team to continue the Airstream heritage and to seek new opportunities. After Stella's death, both Costello and Charles bought up large blocks of stock from Stella's estate, and a few of the directors bought some.

Charles was underemployed in his new position, so he decided to head up an Around the World Caravan, while Costello remained behind to manage the business. After the caravan returned, it was only a matter of time before Charles left his chairmanship, though exactly when he exited the company is unclear. It was really too bad: he was a good man and he'd done a lot for Airstream. In the clash of personalities and management styles, though, there was no possibility of a truce.

OPERATION SURVIVAL

Costello began to leave his imprint on Airstream, Inc. as soon as he took control. He'd been studying the travel trailer market and had formed certain opinions about its direction—and what tactics Airstream should employ in response. Convinced that the market was about to turn downward, Costello moved to head off the expected drop in revenue by launching a wide-reaching initiative called "Operation Survival." This was a fully formed, meticulous plan to expand Airstream into new markets and develop new income streams while leveraging the brand's inherent strengths, especially its brand name and iconic image. Part of Costello's plan was to reduce overhead by cutting office expenses as well as production costs, while at the same time raising revenues through new income opportunities to be developed by the company.

In one of the first implementations of "Operation Survival," Airstream introduced the Wally Byam Stores, a concept that evolved into retail operations run by

These two macho guys are, left to right, actor Keenan Wynn and Olympian Bob Mathias, who costarred in the exciting television series, *Troubleshooters*, about men who work on far-flung construction jobs around the globe, living and working out of an Airstream trailer. The show ran from 1959 to 1960. Keenan Wynn, son of actor Ed Wynn, is perhaps best known for his role as Col. "Bat" Guano in the dark comedy *Doctor Strangelove*.

Top: President John F. Kennedy inspects Airstream-built mobile hospital units at the White Sands Missile Range in New Mexico in 1963. The Air Force used several of these units.

Bottom left: Taken around 1963, this photo shows an Airstream family enjoying the view of Niagara Falls from the Canadian side. Canada has always been a popular destination for Airstream caravans, since it offers beautiful scenery as well as a diverse culture. Quebec Province offers a truly "foreign" experience, with a different language and culture than other parts of Canada. Visits to Old Montreal and Quebec City are especially enjoyable.

Bottom right: Another view of the Air Force Mobile Hospital units built on Airstream chassis. Note the Pontiac ambulance parked to the right.

Taken in Singapore Harbor in 1963, this photo shows the local stevedores unloading Airstream trailers for their journey there.

The always-popular Ford Country Squire station wagon was another ideal tow vehicle in the 1960s and 1970s. This 1967 model is towing an Airstream in beautiful Hawaii.

Airstream dealers. These stores sold trailer accessories and parts, including trailer polish, couch cushions, bed pillows, and specially designed travel cups and dinnerware, along with all the sundry little aids that Wally and his team had developed over years of travel and testing. The stores were a hit, providing the corporation with a healthy new profit center and income stream.

Part of this success was grounded in Airstream's hard-won reputation for product innovation. Among the firsts it could claim in the travel trailer field was the first holding tank, the first ladder-type frame, and the first pressurized water system. Costello put renewed emphasis on product innovation, introducing a substantial improvement in trailer suspensions—the new Dura-Torque axle system, which used sturdy rubber torsion bars cradled in rubber instead of old-fashioned leaf or coil springs. The torsion bars provided better cushioning against road shock, reducing pitch and jounce, as well as delivering substantial improvements in noise, vibration, and harshness (NVH) factors. The ride and handling benefits were far and away superior to every other trailer on the road. Airstream engineers also developed a new

After losing out on the chance to become president of Airstream in 1963, Andy Charles decided to take his wife on an already-planned Airstream trip, the famous Around the World Caravan. This press photo shows Charles, in classic blue beret, snuggling up with a friendly elephant that belonged to the Maharajah of Benares, India.

CATCH THE BIG ONE WITH AN AIRSTREAM

Right: Look closely at this magazine cover and you can spot Charles's Ford pickup, this time in front of the Tombs of the Seven Qutub Shahi Kings, in Hyderabad, India.

Opposite: We can spot Charles's Ford pickup and Airstream trailer parked in front the Charminar, a fabulous building in Hyderabad, India, built in 1591. Charminar means "four towers" in the Urdu language.

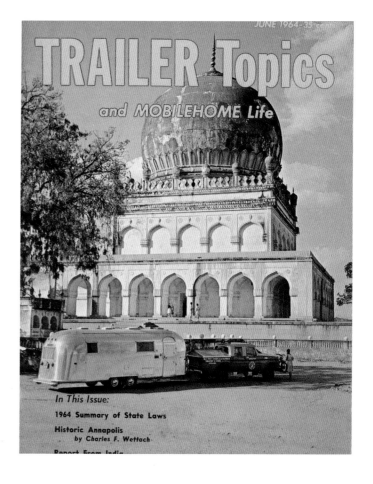

JUNE 1964 35

TRAILER Topics

and MOBILEHOME Life

In This Issue:
1964 Summary of State Laws
Historic Annapolis
   by Charles F. Wettach
Report From India

Uni-Volt electrical system capable of converting 110-volt power from an outside source into several different types used in a trailer, such as 12-volt DC power for light fixtures and 18-volt AC power for fan motors.

Beginning in 1964, Costello focused more intensely on dealer service and parts sales, further upgrading his dealer network and encouraging them to push for more service work and more business in the parts and accessories sector. Dealers added to their repair shops, sent technicians to training classes, and soon were bringing in more revenue on repair work than ever before. Sales of Airstream parts and factory-approved accessories climbed.

Two years later, Airstream entered the lucrative insurance business with a new subsidiary called Caravanner Insurance, Inc. The unit was a property and casualty insurance agency, selling liability and property damage coverage to Airstream owners. Their rates were so good, the company explained, because industry underwriting experience had shown that losses on Airstream trailers were much less than the industry average for travel trailers—proof of the durability of the Airstream product. These insurance policies were sold through licensed Airstream dealers, who worked on commission.

Under Costello, advertising expenditures rose with corporate sponsorship of a new marketing program, "Caravanorama," which was a traveling caravan: a road show of Airstream products that crossed the country on tour. Designed to show off the many innovative features of Airstream trailers, the show included a big fixture that could hold a full-size Airstream on a rotating "spit," useful for showing off the trailer's aerodynamic structure, strongly built framework, and smooth undercarriage.

Nearby was a miniature wind tunnel used to demonstrate the aerodynamic efficiency of Airstream versus other trailers, while a stress tester showed off the strength of Airstream's monocoque (unitized) construction. There was even a miniature model of Airstream's unique Dura-Torque suspension system demonstrating how the trailer's famed stability was achieved.

As promised, Costello reduced corporate expenses, while at the same time allocating money to the Wally Byam Foundation, a nonprofit volunteer organization set up in 1963 to honor the founder. The intent of the foundation was to further international understanding and goodwill through the humanitarian projects it would fund.

Still hungry for additional sales dollars, Costello opened up Airstream to new ideas. One of these was to look for large specialty orders from corporations.

Airstream landed a contract to build fifty custom-designed 38-foot trailers for Southern Pacific Railroad, whose line crews would use them as living quarters. These trailers were larger than the standard Airstream products.

In the end, Costello was wrong about the direction of the trailer market. After a brief hiccup, it continued its strong growth: increasing by 12 percent in 1965 and by 15 percent in 1966. Since Airstream had trimmed down its operations while expanding its range of businesses, the company enjoyed a well-deserved period of prosperity. By 1966, the company's annual sales had grown to

Left: While on the road to Katmandu, Nepal, this Airstream adventurer stopped to take photos of the Palung Valley in Nepal— quite a way from home!

Bottom: These lucky Airstream caravaners visit the Parthenon in Athens, Greece, on a spectacular day.

Does life get any better than this? Airstreaming out west with a 1963 Studebaker Avani as tow car.

$20 million, up from $13 million four years earlier. Expectations now were that the travel trailer market would double between 1966 and 1970. These were golden days indeed for Airstream, Inc.

AIRSTREAM GOES PUBLIC

During 1966, Costello and the Airstream board of directors looked into the idea of taking the company public via an initial public offering (IPO) of stock. In many ways this was a good idea: the company was strong and healthy, the travel trailer market continued to grow, and the company's valuation was excellent. Going public would also give the company better access to capital markets to fund additional growth while strengthening the company's balance sheet. Relatedly, such a move would benefit Costello

personally, since he owned a significant amount of the company's stock. The board decided the time was right and registered for an IPO in July of that year. More than 600,000 shares were issued.

Thus 1966 became the first fiscal year for the newly public Airstream, Inc. The president bragged of his corporation's record gross dollar sales of $20 million, resulting in a net profit of $858,613, which was up a reported 54 percent from the previous year. For all the bragging, however, a closer examination shows the gross profit margin was only about 4.3 percent, and that during a period of the company's greatest sales ever.

Sales continued to rise in 1967, which attracted unexpected attention in the form of corporate suitors looking to buy Airstream. The two most interested were Chris Craft, a well-known maker of powerboats, and,

Top: For those with less time, a quick trip to Florida was always an easy choice to make. Imagine parking your trailer right on the beach, with sand and palm trees all around you. The white sports car barely visible to the right is an early 1960s Fiat.

Right: Same Florida beach, same Airstream Land Yacht, and even the same people, this time photographed from the shore looking out to the water. We love the sentiment in the ad's title: "*You* can be a playboy with an Airstream."

SUNNING, SWIMMING, UNDERWATER FISHING ON THE BEACH

YOU CAN BE A PLAYBOY WITH AN AIRSTREAM!

Everything you do is more fun with an Airstream Land Yacht – skin diving, fly casting, water skiing, camera hunting, even plain old sun-loafing. Just knowing you can go anywhere any*when* makes all the difference between living and livin'. Your Airstream is scientifically engineered and precision built just for travel; utterly luxurious and care-free travel completely independent of outside sources wherever you go, season after season, year after year. You owe it to yourself and to those you love to find out about Land Yachting. Play it cool this summer. Play it warm next winter. Go Airstream.

oddly enough, Beatrice Companies. Both firms made solid offers to acquire Airstream from its stockholders.

Beatrice was the more interested suitor, though Chris Craft was probably a better fit in terms of its product line: like Airstream, it was a longtime player in the leisure/recreational industry. Chris Craft makes high-quality boats primarily for the recreational industry, and, like Airstream, it's an American icon.

On the other hand, Beatrice Companies is a conglomerate best known for its foods division. At the time, though, Beatrice was interested in diversifying itself into other industries, and the company had plenty of cash to back up its expansion goals. In the end, this was the company that landed the coveted Airstream, Inc.

The sale took place in July of 1967, and it made Costello a wealthy man. He maintained his position as president of Airstream, with longtime employee Charles H. Manchester elevated to vice president. Manchester was a solid choice for the job; he'd been with Airstream for many years and was a hard-working, dedicated employee. In the 1950s, Manchester had worked on increasing and improving Airstream's dealer network and did such a good job that, in 1961, he was rewarded with the position of national director of sales and marketing. Since that time he'd been one of the driving forces behind Airstream's continuing sales growth. Costello chose to continue to run Airstream from the California facility's offices.

Beatrice bought Airstream for the purpose of meeting clear strategic goals: its board of directors believed that the travel trailer market was still growing and that it would see its greatest growth in the coming decade. After completing the purchase, they set about supplying the substantial capital that Airstream would need to boost production, modernize plant equipment, processes, and tooling, and invest in better quality control, all the while upgrading the materials and features available on Airstream products.

Beatrice's board also had a big new project in mind.

CARAVAN THE USA IN A SAFER WAY

For 1966, Airstream introduced tempered safety glass in its trailers' front windows. Reportedly ten times the cost of ordinary flat glass panes, this new feature offered safer glass that would crumble into small, granular chunks rather than jagged pieces when broken. In addition, tempered glass is about five times stronger than ordinary glass, so it's less likely to break in the first place. Other improvements this year included molded fiberglass interior walls for a neater, tidier look, Formica countertops, and modernized bathrooms.

Another warm-weather scene, probably Florida, this time with a fun-loving family as the central theme. Mom and the kids get to play in the sand or go swimming, and Dad gets to have his rest.

A BRAND-NEW AIRSTREAM

"Let's not make changes, let's only make improvements." That's what Wally said on more than one occasion, and for many years that's exactly what he and his team had done. But by the late 1960s, the basic Airstream trailer design had been on the market for several decades, much too long if the company hoped to retain its lead in product innovation. Its new corporate parent could secure the necessary funding for a design leap, so management decided it was time for a completely redesigned Airstream that would reflect the best ideas in the recreational vehicle (RV) business.

Left: "Time for tea in Holland." This postcard scene was taken during one of Airstream's numerous caravans to Europe. Airstream travelers found the Dutch to be especially friendly to American tourists, as memories of American soldiers and their sacrifices in liberating Europe during World War II were still fresh in their minds.

Bottom: Another demonstration of Airstream's light yet sturdy monocoque (unitized) construction is seen in this 1965 postcard, taken outside the factory, though whether it was in California or Ohio is not noted.

AIRSTREAM FACTORY, 1965

This unidentified photo from Airstream's corporate archives was taken in Alaska, sometime in the mid-1960s, as the car is a 1963 Ford Country Squire.

St. Basil's Cathedral in Moscow, Russia. One way to identify unmarked photos is to determine the year of the vehicles shown. In this case, though, all that can be said is that it was taken in the 1960s.

Costello put his engineers to work designing and engineering an all-new, state-of-the-art travel trailer from the ground up. Everything was to be new and improved, better than ever before.

The redoubtable Jack Oakley, head of Airstream production, led this new project. Oakley had his team employ automotive methods for product development, where clay models are constructed to refine and develop exterior shapes and surfaces.

The team created mockups of exterior designs until they hit on the best shape, one that would allow greater interior room without altering Airstream's iconic aerodynamic "silver bullet" styling too radically. The frame, which had been redesigned just a few years earlier, was widened to handle a body shell that was now a foot longer and 4 inches wider, yielding much greater interior space. The exterior was even more streamlined than before, and all exterior vents and miscellaneous projecting items were smoothed over and integrated into the exterior surface. The tempered glass front windows took on an attractive wraparound style. The interior

Top: International trucks were favorites of Airstream owners; here we see that Airstream trailers were a favored prop in International's ads. This ad for the 1966 International Travelall illustrates why the two vehicles were a natural match.

Right: Taken around 1966, this photo shows a 1960 Ford pulling a small Airstream trailer near the "singing sand dune," situated 20 miles east of Fallon, Nevada. The dune is 2 miles long and 600 feet high. The sand originates from the ancient Lake Lahontan, which dried up some 9,000 years ago.

An early 1960s-era Ford Falcon pulls a bright shiny Airstream on a winter's journey.

AIRSTREAM – THE BETTER WAY TO TRAVEL

Opposite: Talk about class! These lucky folks owned an Airstream *and* a 1966 Ford Thunderbird.

Bottom: This August 1966 cover of *Trail-R-News* magazine is another photo of an Airstream trailer in Alaska, though it is not the same vehicle seen above. This Airstream is a two-axle vehicle, while the other one had only a single axle. Note how even the background scene is nearly identical, though they appear to have been taken at different times of the year.

50c

Trail-R-News

August 1966
ZONE 11

The complete Mobile Home and Travel Trailer magazine

Show Time in Elkhart!

OUR 49th STATE—Part II

saw all-new designs featuring aircraft-style vinyl-clad aluminum panels, a fiberglass bathroom with shower, convenient tambour-style cabinet doors, and thick shag carpeting.

Introduced in 1969, the all-new Airstream trailers were a big hit, attracting many new customers to the brand as well as many existing customers who chose to trade in so they could experience the new width, length, and greater interior comfort of the new vehicles.

Of course, 1969 was also the year that America landed the first man on the moon. Though Neil Armstrong's first step remains one of mankind's greatest achievements, Airstream actually played a part in his journey, as it did with many other NASA space missions. The company supplied a "mobile quarantine facility," a custom-built Airstream trailer designed with special seals so that the astronauts could be comfortably quarantined upon their return from space. Although the moon was believed to be an airless,

THE NEW AIRSTREAM Bambi

NOW, FOR THE FIRST TIME,
A TRAVEL TRAILER MADE ESPECIALLY FOR SMALL CARS

Top: The most popular small car of the 1960s was Germany's VW Beetle, such as the Karmann-built convertible shown here. For these small, underpowered cars, the Bambi was a godsend, a trailer light enough for even small cars to tow with ease.

Left: This early 1960s Mercedes-Benz would have had plenty of power to haul any Airstream, but its light weight would have made it impractical for the largest trailers.

lifeless satellite, no one could be completely certain there weren't "moon germs" lurking on or below the moon's surface. The earthly quarantine was designed to protect the population from such contamination. President Richard M. Nixon greeted the space travelers on their return as they huddled around a window in the Airstream.

Under the continuing management of Art Costello, Airstream further upgraded its business with the establishment of a formal Research & Development department in Sidney, Ohio, a town that boasted a four-story Airstream office building not far from the Jackson Center factory. Construction also began on an all-new factory across the street from the

The Ford Falcon was an especially popular American-built compact car in the 1960s. It provided decent room and performance along with great fuel economy at a base price starting at $1,912 for a 1960 two-door sedan. This scene was reportedly shot in 1964 and shows a Falcon with a shiny new Bambi.

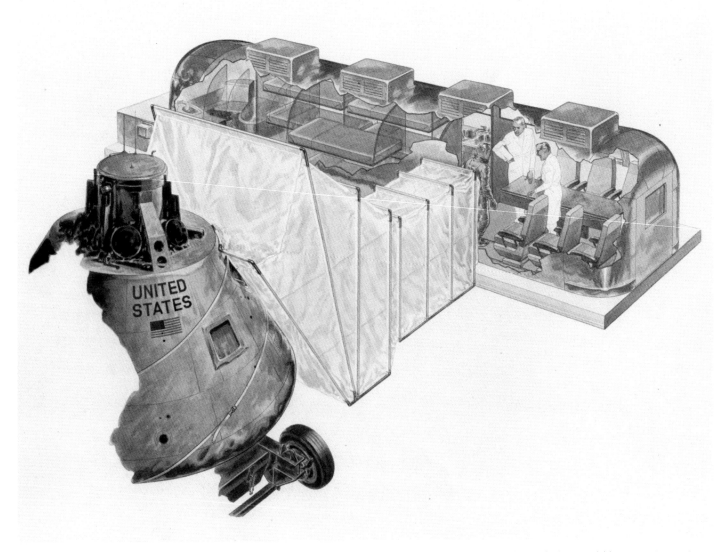

In the mid-1960s, Airstream was approached by NASA to come up with ideas for a special quarantine unit that could house astronauts returning from the moon, a journey President John F. Kennedy had hoped would take place before the end of the decade. This concept drawing was one idea that was advanced.

existing facility, on land that Wally had purchased in 1959 when it was still inexpensive. Put into service in 1971, the new factory was considered the most modern travel trailer plant in the world at the time. At 150,000 square feet, it was certainly big. Airstream retained ownership of the former factory complex, which had grown around the original bazooka plant (see the story in chapter 3). After all, the building wasn't too old for service as storage or as a facility for making components. The company also purchased an

additional 14 acres of land in Jackson Center next to the new factory for any future expansion needs.

Looking for a change, Costello began an orderly transfer of management around the middle of 1970. He was only in his early fifties, but he had become preoccupied with other projects and wanted to get away from the day-to-day running of Airstream so he could focus more on long-term strategy and visit Airstream dealers. Costello began to transfer some of his responsibilities to his vice president. By March 1971,

continued on page 117

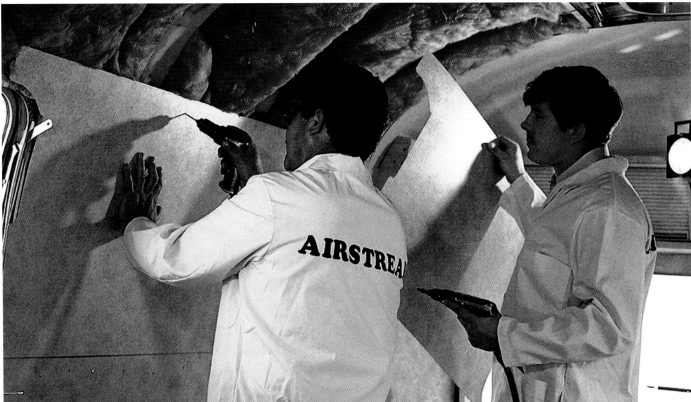

Top: An example of the monocoque construction of a typical Airstream trailer, with a lightweight framework attached to a sturdy undercarriage. This unit, strong all by itself, becomes much stronger when the exterior panels are attached.

Bottom: After exterior walls are attached, workers can install a generous layer of insulation between the structural ribs, along with the vehicle's wiring systems. After this, interior walls can be installed, as shown here. This photo was taken in the mid-1960s.

A completed Airstream from the mid-1960s with the happy family inside. Note the clever skylight over the dining table, providing lots of natural light.

HORNET + 3

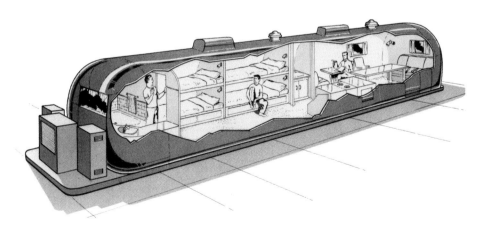

Top: This color photo, taken from aboard the USS *Hornet*, the ship that recovered the returning astronauts after a landing at sea, shows President Richard M. Nixon greeting the three through a window in the actual quarantine unit.

Left: Another drawing of the quarantine vehicle for NASA, this cutaway view illustrates the bunk bed sleeping area, generous bathroom area, and living/dining area that could be provided in such a unit.

Left: This press photo shows an interesting Airstream trailer that was built for the Department of Civil Defense. It was used in an atomic bomb test, which it managed to survive with damage limited to a broken window. The three men pictured are, from left to right, sales executives Virgil Sciullo and Ed Brown and company president Art Costello.

Bottom: Smart travelers know it's wise to plan out each day of a journey, in order to reduce stress and possible mishaps. Here we see an older couple in the mid-1960s planning the day's route. Note the blue berets.

Join an Airstream Wally Byam Caravan for Fun, Friendship and Adventure!

continued from page 112

the transfer was completed and Manchester took full charge of running Airstream as company president—only the third since 1931. Costello retained his position as chairman of the board.

To say that Manchester was grateful to Costello for the opportunity is an understatement. He once declared to others that, "Wally gave us a dream to follow. Art translated that dream into the substance of

continued on page 120

Top: This cute little Bambi is being pulled by an equally cute Rambler American, circa 1965. Bambi's popularity began to wane in the late 1960s, in line with the public's reduced interest in smaller cars. The 1960s horsepower race was on, and car buyers were more inclined to purchase V-8–powered cars, which could tow larger trailers.

Left: When you travel with a Wally Byam Caravan, you're traveling with people who may become your best friends. The camaraderie is always present, and Airstreamers instinctively help one another. There's no better way to travel.

Top: Florida, and all the fun imaginable! Here a circa 1968 Chevy Camaro pulls an Airstream Bambi for two lucky people who are enjoying a day of sun, surf, and scuba diving. By this time, Airstream had been purchased by corporate giant Beatrice, who kept Art Costello in command.

Bottom: The mid-1960s saw a big drop-off in demand for compact cars, as young buyers began purchasing the new "pony cars" in large numbers. These were essentially prettied-up and much sportier compacts, small cars that were more suitable for use with smaller trailers like the Bambi, shown here under the palm trees.

Opposite: Hunting and fishing are a joy when you have an Airstream trailer to return to at the end of the day. This photo, taken in the mid-1960s, features a 1964 Buick Skylark wagon.

Top: Every American should experience the natural beauty of the American West. This lucky couple has set their Land Yacht right next to a clear blue stream where the fishing is great and the scenery is magnificent.

Bottom: The new Airstream trailers were well received by the public, who bought them in increasing numbers. This super-powerful 1969 Dodge Charger R/T would have no problem pulling the attached Land Yacht.

Opposite: For 1969, Airstream introduced an all-new, state-of-the-art travel trailer developed under the direction of Jack Oakley, head of Airstream production. Oakley's team utilized automotive methods of product development, constructing clay models to refine and develop the exterior shape. The team created a new Airstream trailer with greater interior room, without greatly altering Airstream's iconic, aerodynamic "silver bullet" styling.

continued from page 117

a large and successful business organization." Since he was an Ohio native, Manchester decided to situate his headquarters at the Sidney, Ohio, facility. He thus became the first Airstream executive leader to run things from the eastern branch of the company, much to the dismay of the California employees who would eventually feel out of touch with management.

For 1972, the company enjoyed continued success, once again achieving record sales and profits. Costello's succession plan had been timely: less than two years after giving up the reins, he died of a sudden, massive heart attack on December 16, 1972, while doing some Christmas shopping in California. He was only fifty-three years old. At his memorial service, a grieving Manchester called him the man who "was responsible more than any

other man for the prosperity and security our company and each of us . . . enjoy today."

With Manchester firmly in command, Airstream's center of gravity began to shift to Jackson Center and Sidney, Ohio. In time, the engineering department was moved to Ohio, along with the national sales department, warranty department, and more. In relatively short order, Ohio became the focal point of Airstream operations and the California operation dwindled to a mere outpost. Some workers chose not to make the move and left the company. Many of those who remained in California felt disconnected from the company's heartbeat.

Above: In 1970, Chevrolet produced this picture postcard of the new Impala with an Airstream trailer.

Left: A lone traveler on the road with his Airstream, from around 1971, framed by a beautiful rainbow on the horizon.

Below: A young family enjoys a rest stop along their journey.

Airstream's interior designs became increasingly clever and stylish as the 1970s proceeded. These two views feature a typical Airstream trailer from the early 1970s.

THE BIRTH OF ARGOSY

For many years, Airstream had sought entry into the midpriced trailer market. The challenge was to deliver the same quality product at a lower cost, without giving up the handsome profit margins enjoyed by the company or cheapening the Airstream brand. This idea had been on Wally's mind for a long time, and he even managed to field an entry—the long-forgotten, low-cost trailer that everyone said looked like a canned ham—whose passing was lamented by none. Costello had also given the problem serious consideration several times before he passed away. Manchester now saw his chance: he put his engineers to work on developing a new trailer that could play off the Airstream heritage without actually bearing the Airstream brand name, a strategy that he hoped might avoid cheapening the Airstream image.

The result debuted in 1973, with a brand-new division hard at work building a new trailer, the Argosy. There were four distinct models, ranging in length from 20 to 26 feet. To further separate the brands, the new Argosy was built in a separate plant, in Versailles, Ohio, some 36 miles from Jackson Center. To most people, though, the Argosy looked like a painted Airstream trailer. It featured the familiar rounded shape, wraparound front windows, similarly unitized construction with an enclosed underbelly pan, and even Airstream's patented Dura-Torque axle system. This begs the question: where were the cost savings that made a lower price tag viable? The answer is that the savings, though real, weren't all that great.

In part, Argosy's lower cost was made possible by its construction with a lower grade of aluminum, made possible since the all Argosy trailer exteriors were painted. In addition, cost savings were realized by making the front and rear cap sections out of a single piece of stretch-formed steel rather than five sections of formed aluminum. Inside, Argosy's interiors were not as fancy as in the Airstream product, and there were fewer standard features. All this added up to prices that ranged from $3,990 to $5,775, depending on the model, which was up to 20 percent lower than the cost of a comparable Airstream.

Top: Extra-snug insulation and a fine heating system are two of the big advantages an Airstream trailer offers. These combine to make cold-weather touring possible.

Bottom: An Airstream that's not meant for fun. Exactly how many DWI test vans were built is unknown.

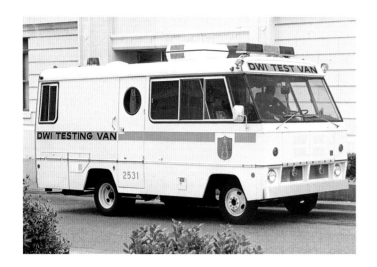

Manchester may have gone too far in his efforts to separate the two trailer brands, though, because acquiring an additional factory—rather than utilizing existing plant space—increased the product's cost. Manchester also had a separate crew of executives running Argosy, which also increased costs. All of these added expenses had to be figured into each Argosy trailer's price, making it vital that the new division sell enough of its products. If volume production couldn't be maintained, the new division would begin to lose money.

In an effort to keep the brands separate, Airstream, Inc. decided that Argosy purchasers would not be

continued on page 128

The Oldsmobile Toronado coupe was a good tow vehicle, with front-wheel drive that provided excellent traction in concert with its huge engine-boosted locomotive torque. This 1973 Oldsmobile Toro is parked outside the Leaning Tower of Pisa in Italy.

Opposite top: Always a popular tourist destination, Taos, New Mexico, gives visitors a look at an ancient civilization, with local Native Americans on hand to introduce newcomers to the Pueblo Indian culture. This photo was taken in the mid-1970s.

Opposite bottom: During 1972, the company enjoyed great success, once again achieving record sales and profits. But in December 1972, Art Costello died suddenly while doing some Christmas shopping in California. He was only fifty-three years old. The cause of death, a massive heart attack. Control of the company was turned over to Chuck Manchester.

Top: Not every trip is to a remote landscape. This photo, taken in San Francisco near the Golden gate Bridge in 1972, shows the elegance that Airstream has brought to what used to be known as "camping" but is really journeying by trailer.

Right: The great American West, where you can still see Native Americans in their traditonal dress, with displays of their enormous teepees. The owners of the lovely Airstream Land Yacht have stopped to take some pictures for the folks back home, who apparently weren't as adventurous as our intrepid Airstream owners.

This page and next: No matter the location, season, or company, Airstream offered something for everyone.

continued from page 124

eligible to participate in Airstream rallies or the Wally Byam Caravan Club. This was clearly a mistake, since it had the potential to make Argosy owners feel like second-class citizens, resentful of the Airstream owner group. Although an Argosy owners club was set up to accommodate that group, this did little to reduce the disappointment consumers felt at being restricted from official Airstream activities.

With its bright new Argosy lineup to lure new buyers to the company—and the enduring beauty of the Airstream line always there to attract those wanting only the best—Airstream seemed to be riding high at the beginning of 1973. During this peak year of the 1970s, Airstream stood ready to expand beyond anything yet imagined. Manchester gazed into his crystal ball with great satisfaction: the future looked bright indeed.

Top right: Airstream tried to appeal to progressive¨ jet-setting-on-the-ground¨ homemakers with ads like this one.

Left, bottom right, and opposite: Coast to coast and everywhere in between, Airstream meant to open up the world to its customers. And they did.

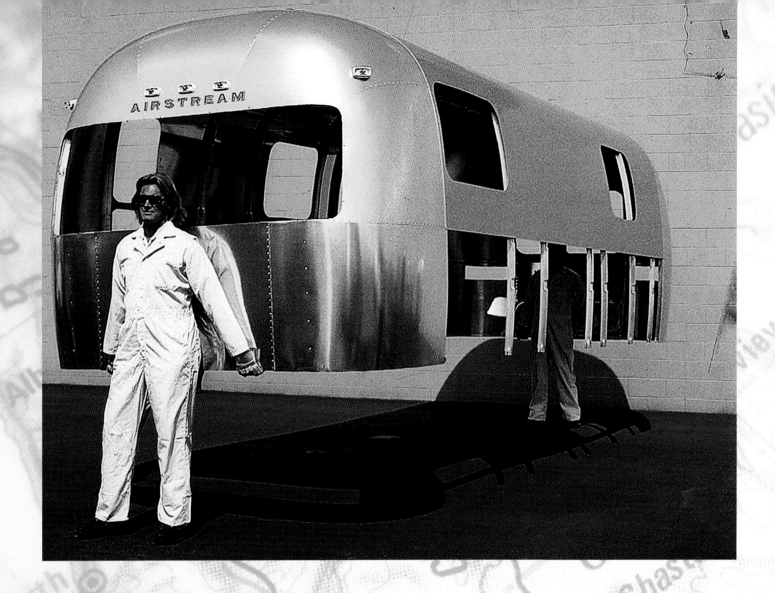

CHAPTER FIVE

CRISIS AND RECOVERY: 1973–1982

The 1970s had started out on a strong note, and sales of travel trailers—especially Airstreams—grew smartly with each year. The company had been led by talented people and prospered, leveraging its iconic image and reputation for quality to bring new customers on board and continually building up its production capacity to meet the growing demand.

Opposite: The lads at Airstream were always ready to provide a demonstration of their products' lightweight yet sturdy monocoque construction. Two men hold the entire body shell for a midsize Airstream trailer without difficulty. Note that the structure remains rigid, despite being picked up.

Bottom: In this aerial photograph, taken during a Homecoming Rally at the Jackson Center plant campus, the large one-story building in the lower right—actually four building placed side by side—is the former bazooka plant that once served as the main plant for Airstream's Ohio production facility. The large blue building at the top center is the big new main plant. The older plant now produces Airstream Interstate motor coaches.

For 1973, Airstream, Inc. had its new Argosy brand, which was designed to bring even more new customers into the Airstream family. No one doubted that Argosy would be a hit. After all, it was designed by the same people who over a long period of time had created many other successful travel trailers, and the new Argosy had the backing of the greatest travel trailer organization in the world. Still, some people questioned the wisdom of Airstream moving into the lower price market.

The question of Airstream's wisdom in attempting to enter this market, to say nothing of how viable Argosy could have been had external market forces not blocked its growth, remains open to this day. It was a fine product that could compete readily with other medium-priced brands. Buyers were well aware of Airstream's design expertise, which they valued greatly.

Top: Yacht owners could take comfort knowing they could lock up home right next to the yacht!

Right: Under the palm trees in Florida, 1970s. As the decade progressed from 1970 to 1973, Airstream went from success to success, with demand for its products growing, seemingly with no end in sight.

Nevertheless, the new Argosy failed to boost company sales in any significant way. The reason was not due to any inherent defects or flaws in the product, but rather because in October 1973, mere months after its introduction, the Organization of Petroleum Exporting Countries (OPEC) proclaimed an oil embargo against the United States and other countries in retaliation for their support of Israel during the recent Yom Kippur War. The result was utter catastrophe for the US economy: oil prices quadrupled almost overnight from $3 to $12 a barrel, and fuel shortages became the norm across America. Long lines soon formed at gas stations as millions of desperate car owners tried to obtain fuel that had suddenly become scarce. There were fistfights in gas lines, a few fatal shootings, and an abrupt and long-lasting slump in

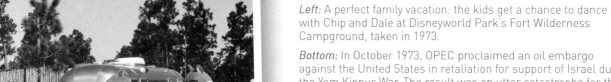

Left: A perfect family vacation: the kids get a chance to dance with Chip and Dale at Disneyworld Park's Fort Wilderness Campground, taken in 1973.

Bottom: In October 1973, OPEC proclaimed an oil embargo against the United States in retaliation for support of Israel during the Yom Kippur War. The result was an utter catastrophe for the US economy, as oil prices quadrupled to $12 per barrel and fuel shortages sprang up all across America. Panicked drivers waited for hours in long lines at gas stations trying to obtain fuel for their vehicles. Naturally, sales of big cars fell rapidly, as did sales of travel trailers.

economic activity. Tens of thousands of people lost their jobs as economic activity quickly evaporated. In the end, this was considered the most disruptive single event in the national economy since the Great Depression.

Sales in nearly all sectors dropped dramatically. Big-ticket items were the worst hit, with sales of automobiles, trucks, and every kind of leisure vehicle (including boats and RVs) plummeting. Industry sales of travel trailers fell an amazing 50 percent in just two years. At Airstream, orders slowed to a crawl. With his sales background, Manchester probably believed he could sell his way out of the situation, but the problems he faced were greater than he realized. With inventory piling up at Airstream's factories, parent company Beatrice was forced to step in and order a complete shutdown of Airstream production

plants for nearly four months to work off the excess trailer stock on hand. Airstream was hemorrhaging, and the company needed a tourniquet.

NEW PRODUCTS

In response to this crisis, Manchester put his engineering team to work developing new products that he hoped would diversify the company sufficiently to reduce dependence on its core business. Manchester was under pressure from his corporate bosses at Beatrice, and he believed the only way to save the company was to get it back to work building products, even if they were in markets far outside Airstream's competence to produce.

These new products included a large commercial delivery truck, the A-van, which was sold to small business users such as bakeries as well as large delivery

Left: With Airstream sales tanking, company president Manchester ordered up a wide range of new products aimed at novel market niches. One of the more ambitious was this delivery truck, a large step van for the package delivery market. Although hundreds of these vehicles were produced, their sales volume wasn't high enough to justify their continuation, and they were dropped.

Right: Seen here while still under development, the Airstream-produced delivery truck, right, next to a standard Olsen (AKA Grumman-Olsen) delivery truck, which coincidentally was also made of aluminum. The Airstream job looks much more attractive and modern, but it was not ultimately successful.

Left: This aluminum Eagle One People Mover was produced by Airstream in an effort to keep its factories busy. Once it was clear that the business model would not be sustainable, the company got out of the market.

Below: With traditional markets still in a funk, Airstream was considering other new products to generate new business. This design sketch shows one idea: a coach-type transporter that could be built as a bus or trailer and used to transport people in solid comfort.

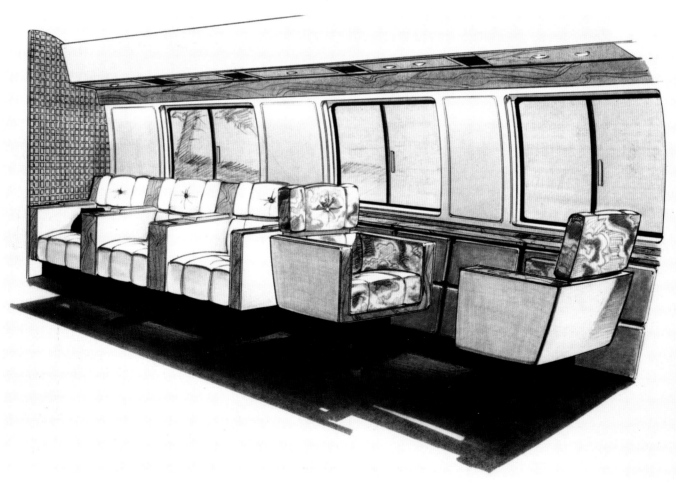

Above: An Airstream vendor trailer, featuring a swing-up side door that doubles as a shade for waiting customers. This particular unit was used for retailing gold and silver jewelry at various outdoor events.

Right: One of the most attractive Class A motorhomes of all time. This Airstream 310 from the late 1970s featured a powerful engine and all the luxury amenities that are synonymous with the Airstream name and image.

companies, including UPS and the US Postal Service. Another new product was a line of modern aluminum "people movers," enclosed trams that rode on rail tracks. These were sold to Westinghouse and put into service at the Atlanta International Airport.

As a further move toward diversification, the company introduced a motorhome, the first in company history. Perhaps worried that an Airstream-branded motorhome might offend his loyal customer base, Manchester chose to brand it as an Argosy, which meant slotting this new product in the medium price range rather than in the more profitable upper market along with Airstream-brand

Right: Airstream executives were optimistic about this new product, the Argosy Minibus. Although it was stylish, well built, and fuel efficient, Airstream was competing in a down market against companies that made nothing but small buses and had years of experience, not to mention a lower cost basis.

Below: The exterior view of an Airstream Funeral Coach, circa 1982. Having one vehicle that could take the place of several might have taken off in a different market climate. The flowers went into the rear hatch area, as shown, while the casket went into the side carrier space. Mourners rode inside the spacious passenger compartment, a nicely trimmed space that featured individual seats plus a couch at the rear.

vehicles. Available in 24-foot and 26-foot lengths, the Argosy motorhome offered a choice of V-8 engines. It was a handsome, high-quality product with much to offer, but, with fuel at a premium, sales of motorhomes never took off, and the new line received a tepid response.

Another new product, the all-aluminum Compact Passenger Bus was an attractive, well-finished vehicle with sleek styling and beautiful interior trim. Given a better economic environment, it might have caught on, but competition among small bus makers was intense, and it was impossible to build the sales volume required to turn a profit. The Compact Passenger Bus did, however, provide a platform for another variation. Bizarrely, this was a custom funeral coach that doubled as a coffin carrier. The funeral coach was outfitted with a plush interior and featured a side-mounted access door that opened up to receive the coffin. The idea behind the funeral coach was that a single vehicle could replace the customary limousine, flower car, and hearse.

Airstream introduced the Argosy Fifth-Wheel Trailer in an effort to offset business losses in its core product lines. Designed specifically for being towed by pickup trucks, fifth-wheel trailers use a special wheel-shaped receiver hitch mounted in the truck's bed.

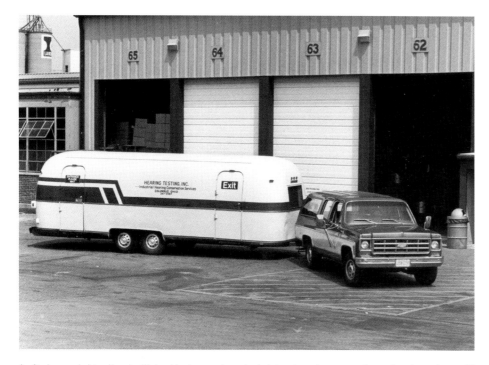

Left: A special trailer built by Airstream to administer hearing tests for school students. The trailer visited schools across the country. At each stop, kids would line up and enter one by one to have their hearing tested on the spot. Hearing Testing, Inc. of Columbus, Ohio, owned and operated this particular unit.

Right: A view inside the special Airstream-built Hearing Testing trailer, providing a mobile, soundproof space for students to have their hearing tested.

Manchester also added a fifth-wheel trailer to the Argosy lineup. Unlike conventional towables that attach to a rear-mounted hitch, a fifth-wheeler has a trailer hitch that attaches to a wheel-like receiver mounted in the bed of a pickup truck.

In addition to new products, Manchester continued building up Airstream's facilities. In response to customer requests, Airstream opened a large new service building constructed next to the new plant in 1974, complete with an Airstream parts and accessories retail store and an attractive customer waiting lounge. This facility remains popular with customers today.

One of Manchester's problems, however, was that he had built up Airstream's facilities too much. The company now had three complete factories, a four-story office building in Sidney, Ohio, the customer center in Jackson Center, the old bazooka plant, test labs, and several other facilities. All of these buildings had to be heated, cooled, and maintained. The facilities were also fully staffed,

creating a large payroll that had to be met every week. Airstream now had a large corporate footprint and costly overhead, threatening the company's ability to turn a profit. The company's scale had increased over the period of years when Airstream was growing fast. With sales in freefall, maintaining its expansive footprint was choking the life out of the company.

None of the new "non-traditional" products proved successful. Although hundreds of A-Vans were sold to UPS and others, and more than 350 of the compact buses and hearses were produced, the products never achieved the volume levels needed for sustainable profitability. According to one Airstream executive, in its rush to get new lines into production, the company had conducted no solid market analysis that would support any of the new products. Though sales were made and the factories had products to build, these new products ultimately weren't profitable, even as they used up Airstream's working capital.

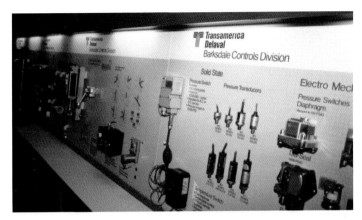

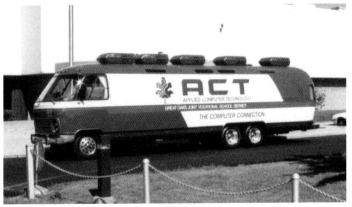

Opposite: Its long-awaited entry into the Class A motorhome business opened up new markets for Airstream. From top to bottom: a Hearing Testing vehicle (sporting a bright color scheme), a Minibus, a Kennedy Space Center shuttle, and a motorhome filled with computer terminals for Applied Computer Technologies, which served various schools.

Top left: In 1974 and 1975, industry sales of travel trailers continued to drop rapidly, an amazing 50 percent in just two years. In response, Airstream promoted its smaller trailers, which could be towed by smaller, more fuel-efficient cars like this 1975 AMC Pacer. The trailer shown is an Argosy, a new brand introduced by Airstream in 1973 to expand its business by offering a lower-priced product.

Top right: The mid-range Argosy trailer, towed by a 1978 Buick wagon, possibly in St. Louis, Missouri. Even though the Argosy models were more reasonably priced and offered many of the advantages of the premium Airstream trailers, their sales were never high. Eventually, the company ended their production to focus on its core brand.

Bottom: The Argosy Compact Bus from the late 1970s. This one was used as an airport shuttle. Argosy buses might have caught on and become successful had the economy been in better shape and competition in the bus business not been as intense. The company eventually discontinue this product line.

Airstream was and had always been a premium travel trailer builder. It lacked the know-how and capacity to compete effectively with companies that had been building trucks and buses for decades. Besides, Manchester hadn't given thought to the idea that his new products were entering markets suffering in much the same way as the travel trailer industry, if not worse. Too many companies were angling for too little business while facing the same profit-killing oversupply.

Airstream continued to lose money in 1975 and 1976. Worse, the company's vaunted quality had also begun to suffer, which was wrecking customer brand loyalty and further jeopardizing sales. Clearly, something had to be done.

Top: The Argosy line of trailers for 1977, with the largest trailer in the front, the smallest in the rear (being pulled by an AMC Pacer). The Argosy was sometimes called the "Painted Airstream" because their overall shapes and construction were so similar.

Bottom left: Another government-destined Airstream Class A vehicle, this one dubbed the Astrovan. It was used to transport astronauts to and from the Space Shuttle.

Bottom right: A space shuttle transporter, seen here in action on the shuttle's landing strip. The extra equipment mounted on what appears to be a raised roof distinguishes this vehicle from the one in the previous photo.

HEMORRHAGING MONEY

By 1977, Airstream was losing *one million dollars a month*, with no end in sight. Beatrice Companies had had enough: they decreed that it was time for a change. Manchester was shown the door, and a new man took the president's chair with orders to fix Airstream's problems, period. Airstream's new leader, an outside consultant named Robert Devine, was known as a tough cost-cutter. He had been given a mission: stop the bleeding by slashing Airstream's cost basis until it was brought in line with revenues.

Devine wasted little time, shuttering the Cerritos, California, plant and laying off its employees, thus ending Airstream's long stay in California. The plant would never reopen. He also closed the office building in Sidney, Ohio, moving its functions to Jackson Center. Devine had decided that Jackson Center would be the focal point of Airstream's slimmed-down operations, so he hired a dozen veteran industry executives to whip the plant and its various departments into shape. They eliminated several tiers of management to cut payroll expenses and

These photos from around 1979 illustrates the inside and outside of the new Airstream Caravelle trailer. It was large enough for plenty of comfort but small enough for a light compact car such as the Ford Fairmont to tow it.

enforce better accountability. Operating costs were cut, and cut again. Sales continued to fall, though, making it impossible for the company to turn a profit. Airstream sales shrank from a high of $70 million in 1972 to $30 million in 1978. By 1979, the decision was made to halt Argosy production, and the plant in Versailles was closed.

Some of Devine's cuts were questionable. To further reduce company expenses, he cancelled the annual Homecoming Rally, a fairly expensive event that was nevertheless highly useful for soliciting new business. Discontinuing Airstream's sponsorship of the Wally Byam Caravan Club International was another tactical error he made. The event was turned over to the club members, which lost the company direct control of another valuable marketing channel.

By this time, Beatrice was considering dropping some of its unprofitable companies, with Airstream, Inc. chief among them. Research into the industry revealed how much money a large RV maker can lose once it tips into loss territory. With no end of losses in sight, Beatrice

Top: Airstream motorhomes were constructed using techniques that were surprisingly similar to trailer construction, as this photo taken at the factory illustrates; here, the front and rear endcaps are being assembled.

Bottom: Airstream can treat you to more of nature's wonders than any resort or luxury hotel can. This scene shows early morning in camp, with a gorgeous double rainbow overhead.

Top: The motorhome endcaps are added to the main body structure. The next step would be to mount this structure onto the main chassis.

Left: Motorhomes and trailers produced by Airstream take a lot of aluminum sheets. For this reason, one of the more important jobs has always been metal forming, as seen here.

began looking for someone to take Airstream off its hands. Unsurprisingly, as industry sales were at an all-time low, no buyers came forward. No one was interested in buying a money-losing trailer manufacturer; no one, that is, until 1980, when two audacious men approached Beatrice about buying their troubled subsidiary.

THE NEW TEAM

The intrepid buyers were Wade F. B. Thompson and Peter Orthwein, partners and owners of a small recreational vehicle firm named Hi-Lo Trailer Company. Hi-Lo made a unique pop-up travel trailer with a sliding hardtop roof that telescoped down for highway travel, then slid upward to provide living space when parked.

Thompson, a born entrepreneur and native of New Zealand, had first spotted Hi-Lo while working as vice president of corporate development for a company in Texas. Seeing an opportunity to buy a solid company at a good price—reportedly less than $1 million—he approached an investment banker, Orthwein, and together they purchased Hi-Lo in October 1977. Orthwein, great-great grandson of the founder of beer-making giant Anheuser-Busch, wanted to participate mainly as an investor, while majority partner Thompson chose to take direct command at Hi-Lo, even though it entailed taking a big cut in his annual salary. Living with his family in New York City, Thompson spent the next three years commuting to Ohio during the week, working every waking moment at Hi-Lo, building it into an even stronger company. Friday evenings he boarded a plane for a flight home to New York so he could spend the weekend with his family, then it was back to Ohio and the hard grind of transforming Hi-Lo into the sort of company he envisioned. Thompson managed it so well that, by 1980, he and Orthwein were ready to expand their business holdings. Looking around for more opportunities in the travel trailer business, they decided to acquire the company both men recognized was "the crown jewel of the industry," Airstream, Inc.

Their initial approach was rebuffed by Beatrice. Six months later, when they again inquired about buying Airstream, Beatrice executives seemed much more

Top: On August 29, 1980, Wade Thompson (left) and Peter Orthwein (right) became the new owners of Airstream, having purchased the company from Beatrice. The company was nearly bankrupt, which allowed the buyers to negotiate a deal with no money down; Beatrice provided the financing.

Opposite: Airstream employees gathered in front of the big main plant in Jackson Center to commemorate the building of the 100,000th Airstream.

receptive. Thompson and Orthwein were invited to Chicago, and they soon found themselves sitting down with a couple of top managers at Beatrice, working out a deal.

It was a good time to make a pitch for Airstream. In the terrible economic climate, the company's valuation was at a very low point. At least to Thompson and Orthwein, though, the trailer market appeared ready for a rebound. Because he was so closely in tune with retail orders at Hi-Lo, Thompson could discern a slight increase in business activity within the industry. Orthwein and Thompson believed this indicated it was the perfect time to buy another company in their field.

Their one-day negotiating session in Chicago yielded fruit: on August 29, 1980, the two men became the new owners of Airstream. They had negotiated a rather sharp deal, with no money down and with Beatrice throwing in financing. At the same time, they formed a new parent

Top: As the new owners of Airstream, Thompson and Orthwein set up a new parent firm, Thor Industries, and started planning the acquisition of other RV firms. The name "Thor" comes from the first two letters of the owners' last names.

Bottom: This looks like New England, but really it could be just about anywhere in the United States. A happy couple enjoys their new Airstream Limited. Note the skylight over the dining area.

company called Thor Industries, creating the company's name by using the first two letters of each man's last name. Thor Industries would concentrate its efforts on acquiring other companies in the recreational vehicle field, leveraging its core competencies to grow the businesses. Orthwein became chairman of Thor, with Thompson serving as president.

Reviving Airstream was a long shot in August 1980. Even after all the cost-cutting and budget slashing, the company had lost $2.5 million from March 1 to August 31 that year, after suffering a disastrous 1979 fiscal year. Once the deal was signed, though, Thompson and Orthwein were elated—they knew in their hearts that they had landed a once-in-lifetime opportunity. They would rebuild Airstream, Inc. and restore the company to glory and profitability.

Since Orthwein wouldn't be involved in the day-to-day management of Airstream, Thompson set about building

a new management team. He elevated Airstream's Executive Vice President Gerry Letourneau to president. Letourneau was a young but experienced executive and a dynamic personality. He loved the outdoors and enjoyed camping in his trailer or snowmobiling on nearby lakes and trails. Other executives on the team included Walter Bennett as chief financial officer, Larry Huttle as vice president of sales, and Rex Miner, vice president of product development. From the start, Thompson told all of his executives that the days of using red ink in the business ledgers were over. Their job was to make Airstream profitable.

The new team quickly went to work reducing manufacturing costs while also improving the product's design by adding more windows to the trailer fronts. Although Devine's team had done a good job of slashing costs at Airstream, Thompson saw many more expenses that could be reduced or eliminated. He began to cut Airstream's overhead even further, a necessity since the company's annual sales had fallen to less than

Below left: Any Airstream product will offer a comfortable bed and plenty of natural light. Note the desktop in the rear of the vehicle, complete with a built-in overhead lamp.

Below right: The living area of this Airstream trailer boasts a full sofa with storage underneath and a movable chair. The oven with full cooktop is visible in the foreground.

Bottom: On the road again—the same could be said for Airstream following its purchase by Orthwein and Thompson. Thompson was the hands-on manager, living in Jackson Center during the week and traveling home to New York City only on the weekends. His tireless efforts soon worked to turn around the foundering company.

$23 million in 1979; costs simply had to be brought under control to get them lower than revenues.

Thompson also put renewed focus on quality, improving manufacturing processes and making sure dealer orders were shipped as soon as they were completed in order to free up capital. One of the first things Thompson investigated was the large increase in Airstream warranty costs that had crept in over the years. He discovered that many dealers were submitting fraudulent or inflated claims. Coming down hard on these costs, Thompson was able to cut $1 million out of the company's warranty expenses.

To make sure the firm's executives remained focused on the fundamentals of the business, he also created what he called a daily report of operations, which was used to track sales, production, and, most importantly, cash flow. Thompson also reinstated the annual Airstream Homecoming Rally, which had always been a valuable tool for receiving feedback from customers as well as an opportunity to win new business from them.

Thompson was absolutely correct about the market coming back. Airstream's annual sales increased to $26 million in 1980, with a net profit of $1 million. This was followed by another decent year, and 1982 was even better. With the ship righted and back on course, it was time to begin planning for the future. Thompson finally returned to live in New York, where he could manage Thor Industries rather than just one of its companies. He left Airstream in the care of his handpicked executive team. Before he departed, though, he gave them a bit of advice. "Happiness," he told them, "is a full order backlog and positive cash flow."

Going forward, Thompson would work with Orthwein to build Thor Industries into a powerhouse company, eventually making it the top firm in the RV business. By acquiring other recreational vehicle companies and then working diligently to improve each company's operations, the firm was able to achieve and maintain sustainable profits. Airstream's fate was in the hands of Gerry Letourneau, Larry Huttle, Walter Bennett, and Rex Miner, its best team in years.

Right: Letourneau, president of Airstream on January 5, 1982, seated in one of the Airstream funeral coaches.

Below: A pair of big International Series Airstreams.

CHAPTER SIX

ON THE MOVE AGAIN

When he left Jackson Center for New York, Wade Thompson left behind a team of executives he knew and trusted. He'd worked closely with them over the difficult months as they turned Airstream around, so he knew he could leave them alone and trust them to continue the company's transformation. He left them empowered to make the right decisions that would grow the business profitably.

Top: A nice view of an Airstream interior from 1983, showing lots of living space and a cabin with a bright, airy feel. Sales were picking up at Airstream as the US economy slowly began to improve.

Left: The Airstream 270 Class A motorhome was a popular model during the 1980s. Business continued to improve as industry sales climbed from a low of less than 107,000 units in 1980 to over 215,000 units in 1984. Thompson and Orthwein were able to pay off the balance owed Beatrice for buying the company a few years earlier.

For the most part, the team worked harmoniously. Letourneau was a manufacturing expert. Huttle, Bennett, and Miner concentrated on their own jobs and didn't get involved in turf wars, unlike the old days under Costello and Charles. Business continued to improve. Industry sales rocketed from a low of less than 107,000 units in 1980 to over 215,000 units in 1984, and trends were pointing to even higher sales in the next few years. Airstream continued to generate profits. In short order, Thompson and Orthwein were able to pay off their debt to Beatrice even as they worked diligently to acquire other RV makers and fold them into Thor Industries. To grow the company further, they decided to take Thor public.

Under Letourneau's direction, the Jackson Center plant further refined its processes, reducing manufacturing costs even as quality was improved. In addition, he renewed the company's emphasis on developing new products. Unlike the previous unsuccessful attempts, however, this time the products would be complementary to the Airstream product line. The company wouldn't attempt to build trucks, vans, buses, hearses, or people movers. Its product lines would remain strictly within the core RV business.

One surprising project the team undertook was a revival of the Argosy brand, which had been dormant since it was dropped in 1979. Airstream's managers

Top: The companies that made high-end sport utility vehicles liked to show their products with the finest trailers in the world, as Jeep did in this 1985 press photo for the ultra-luxurious Grand Wagoneer. The big Jeep was a nautral tow vehicle for the Airstream, with four-wheel drive, a big V-8 engine, and acres of luxury within.

Bottom: This Airstream participated in the 1985 Caravan to China, one of the most ambitious caravans to date.

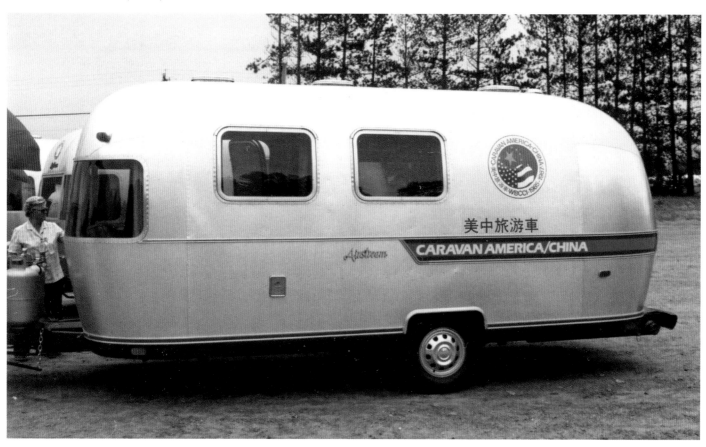

This mid-1980s Airstream Land Yacht represented the company's attempt to play off the Land Yacht motorhome's success by rebadging an Argosy trailer as an Airstream. The vehicle's rectangular shape didn't endear it to hardcore Airstream loyalists, though, and its sales were disappointing.

realized that, although it may have been necessary to discontinue Argosy during the downturn, the company was still missing an entry-level product to introduce new generations of owners to the Airstream family. The Airstream dealer network had long realized the need. Airstream sales alone couldn't support overhead, which had led dealers to offer medium-priced trailers and motorhomes from Holiday Rambler and other firms.

Simply reintroducing the old Argosy line would not be enough, though—too many years had passed. A completely reengineered lineup was created, with squarer shapes that provided greater interior space as well as visually distancing Argosy from the Airstream product. The new version also featured greater use of fiberglass and bonded aluminum. For the sake of continuity, the trademark Argosy beige and cream color scheme was retained. The new Argosy models were introduced for 1986. Two years later, they were joined by a new Argosy fifth-wheel trailer.

The story of successes in this period ended on a bittersweet note. The Airstream family faced another tragedy in January 1988. While riding out at Indian Lake with friends, company President Gerry Letourneau, an avid outdoorsman, lost control of his snowmobile and hit a pile of rocks. Letourneau died of head injuries suffered in the crash. He was fifty-two years old.

HUTTLE TAKES COMMAND

The loss of Letourneau left a huge gap in Airstream's management team, and Thompson and Orthwein were not certain how to fill it. Months went by before they announced a new president. On October 4, 1988, after reviewing all his options, Thompson promoted Sales Vice President Larry Huttle to the presidency of Airstream. Huttle was probably the best choice—he was young, energetic, and aggressive, a hockey player in his youth, and a dynamic sales executive in his automotive and RV career. He'd attended the University of Minnesota and the University of Wisconsin. He began an executive training program with Chrysler Corporation in 1968, later becoming a district sales manager for the Midwest. He then entered the motorhome industry with a major manufacturer before being tapped to come to Airstream.

At Airstream, Huttle's dynamic personality and gregarious nature helped endear him to his colleagues and workers. His undeniable sales expertise went a long way toward helping Airstream rebuild its retail efforts. A genuine enthusiast, Huttle attended dozens of Airstream events in his two Airstream trailers. He was popular with his dealers, who could sense his sincere affection for them as well as his concern for the welfare of their businesses. He was also a strong believer in listening to what customers and dealers said they needed

Top left: This 1986 Airstream's interior is as comfy and plush as a fine hotel. Judging by the handle on the front edge, this sofa pulls out to make a bed, a common touch in Airstream trailers. Note the color-coordinated carpeting.

Top right: Another Airstream interior from 1986, probably in a Land Yacht. Instead of wraparound curtains, we find attractive wooden blinds, an overstuffed couch, and stylish, wall-mounted light fixtures.

Bottom: Known in the industry as a "basement model," this Airstream motorhome features generous storage space underneath its floor. Convenient side hatches open up for access to the "basement."

or wanted in a product, then trying his best to deliver it to them. Huttle believed that such an approach was fundamental to the success of the company.

Huttle was also a stickler for quality. He ordered a further upgrade of Airstream's quality control systems and standards while pressing suppliers to upgrade theirs as well. Product testing now included extensive time at the Transportation Research Center of Ohio, a large independent vehicle testing facility that had the capabilities to do much more precise testing to ensure top product durability for Airstream products. Huttle implemented "just in time" (JIT) inventory management, a technique used by the big automobile companies; this greatly reduced the amount of working capital tied up in inventory.

The company's reputation grew. In 1987, *Money* named Airstream trailers "one of 99 things that Americans make best." Around this time, the company also got into the growing Class B motorhome market with the fiberglass-bodied Airstream B-van, built on a Dodge chassis.

Airstream management took a wild risk in 1989 with the introduction of a new Class A motorhome under the Airstream brand name. Different from anything they had offered before, this big new motorhome featured square-cut body lines, fiberglass construction, and an extended aerodynamic nose section, giving it an appearance unlike conventional Airstream products.

The new motorhome, dubbed the Land Yacht, was an instant success, leading the team to expand its Land Yacht line by rebadging the Argosy trailer as an Airstream

Left: A water-leak test booth at Airstream's Ohio plant.

Bottom: With profits rising, Airstream was able to invest more in quality and performance improvements. This photo, from 1990, shows sophisticated brake testing conducted at the Transportation Research Center of Ohio.

Top left: An interesting idea for an executive people mover, this design includes tables and chairs set up either for face-to-face meetings or relaxing.

Top right: The Airstream-branded Class A motorhomes sold better than the Argosy models ever did. This interior view provides many reasons for the Airstream's success: good design with loads of luxury features. Note the overhead wood cabinets and storage built into the console behind the seats.

Bottom: Exterior view of the 1994 Airstream Land Yacht motorhome, presenting an unusual design that maximizes interior space while providing exterior aerodynamic efficiency, especially in the front.

Land Yacht. "Unfortunately, the rebadged trailer was a misstep: realizing it was really just a gussied-up Argosy, the buying public avoided it. The Land Yacht trailer was dropped in 1991.

Other ideas didn't work out, either. Slide-out trailer models were offered in the 1990s, but demand was low and there were problems with leaks and seals. In time, this design was dropped.

A complete redesign of the basic Airstream trailer platform came in 1994, widened another 5.5 inches to maximize interior space. It was the first major redesign since the big one in 1969. The following year, the Airstream Land Yacht motorhome was also redesigned and widened.

BAMBI RETURNS

For 1998, management decided to revive a once-popular trailer model called the Bambi, which had been Airstream's smallest trailer the 1960s. Originally designed during the period when compact cars were just beginning to grow in popularity, the Bambi was great as a towable for smaller, less powerful cars. In the years

A 1990 model Airstream shown with its proud owners and their Cadillac sedan during an autumn trip. In 1987, *Money* magazine included Airstream trailers as one of its "99 things that Americans make best."

Left: Airstream began producing Class B motorcoaches on both Ford and Chevrolet van chassis in the 1990s. This 1991 Airstream 190 is mounted to a Ford van chassis—a nice little unit.

Bottom: This mid-1990s Airstream 190 is mounted on a Chevy chassis. The roof cap appears to be the same on both the Ford- and Chevy-based products.

All is plush and serene inside the Airstream Land Yacht, with tasteful interior trim, high-quality upholstery, and lots of room. The living room arrangement shown is especially remarkable.

after its unveiling, its popularity had waxed and waned in lockstep with the popularity of compact cars.

The new Bambi was petite and cute as a bug, and it was also many times better than the old one. The little trailer's width was increased, and its interior featured a contemporary interior that included everything anyone needed for camping despite the miniscule overall size. The new Bambi also benefited from the advances in engineering made by Airstream over the years. A high-quality unit perfect for one or two travelers, it proved surprisingly popular, especially with younger people and singles.

The Bambi also benefitted from a new clear-coating process designed to keep the exterior body panels looking shiny and new longer. Developed by Alcoa and PPG, the new coating was applied to the aluminum

sheets by Alcoa during manufacture and then shipped to Airstream, where they were shaped and formed into body panels before installation to the chassis. Use of this new coating was extended to all Airstream trailers.

The 1998 model year also saw an important new design. The company introduced another line, the Airstream Safari, which had been created to provide the company and its dealers with a lower-priced trailer with outstanding appeal. Miner, vice president of product development, developed the concept, featuring a trailer that was 20 percent lighter than a conventional Airstream and easier to tow even with a smaller car. The Safari also cost about 20 percent less, providing more buyers with the opportunity to purchase an Airstream-branded product and, hopefully, expanding Airstream's market.

Top: At the beginning of the 2000s, Airstream offered some of its models with slideout compartments, such as this 34-foot 2000 Limited. Although it enhanced the trailer's interior space, the design didn't work well with the Airstream's rounded shape. Slideouts are better suited to slab-sided vehicles. Additionally, some customers complained of wind noise and water leaks. The factory eventually discontinued offering this line.

Right: An Airstream trailer from around 1995, featuring a like-year Cadillac Fleetwood Brougham on a trip, probably somewhere in the Midwest.

The plan included a more European approach to interior design and furnishings, which management felt would appeal more to younger families.

Although the company had made other efforts to market a lower-priced trailer, none attained the level of success and acceptance that the Safari had. Huttle and Miner had tapped into some long-unfulfilled desire; the Safari was an overnight success, quickly becoming the company's best-selling vehicle. In time it came to represent about half of Airstream's sales volume while winning many new customers to the brand. Buyers loved it.

In 1998, Airstream also welcomed Dicky Riegel as a new member of the executive team. He was a graduate of Vermont's Middlebury College, where he studied art history, studio art, and architecture. As with many art majors, he entered the advertising business, where he spent eight years. Looking for a more lucrative career, he enrolled at Columbia Business School to pursue an MBA in finance and marketing.

He'd married a young woman named Amanda Thompson—whose father just happened to be Thor Industries President Wade Thompson. Not long after Riegel graduated from Columbia, the two attended a New York Rangers game. Thompson turned to his son-in-law and asked him to work for him at Thor. Riegel initially expressed reservations about being a new executive at his father-in-law's company—how it would appear to the other executives there?—but Thompson wouldn't take no for an answer. He knew that Thor needed to start filling and growing its executive ranks with younger people because many of the old-guard executives were nearing retirement age. Miner was nearing retirement, and Huttle wasn't far behind him. Thompson wanted to make sure he had a pool of talent from which to pick the next generation of Thor leaders. Riegel, he felt, had the right combination of skills to become a top-ranking executive one day. Besides, Thompson knew Riegel was someone he could trust—after all, he was family.

The Limited, the most luxurious Airstream produced, even came with folding chairs bearing the Limited name. This older couple look happy as they camp in a lovely spot near a range of majestic mountains.

Top: Although business was good in the 1990s, Airstream contracted to produce bodies for airport shuttles in the same period. This circa-1995 Hertz rental car shuttle was built on a Ford cutaway van chassis.

Bottom: Another Limited, a 1995 model with a slightly different paint scheme.

Riegel started out in a high position at Thor, as vice president of corporate development, a position that allowed him to work closely with Thompson. The idea was that Riegel could learn the business from his father-in-law, who was one of the smartest men in the RV industry. In addition to Airstream, Thor Industries owned Champion Bus, and Riegel worked with Thompson to develop an experimental fuel-cell-powered transit bus that emitted no pollution. After that, they continued working work together on various projects, with Thompson teaching and observing his son-in-law, no doubt grooming him for an even more important future position. It was a significant responsibility: Riegel was in charge of acquiring viable new business, a constant focus of Thompson and Orthwein as they sought to expand Thor.

This 1996 model of an Integrity fifth-wheel trailer represents a new product design for Airstream. These trailers even offered slideout sections that helped increase interior space. Consumers weren't thrilled, and the Integrity was discontinued.

By 1999, Airstream's historic success had been confirmed. Despite extensive investments made to improve product quality and features—and substantial additional costs for testing and development—the company had still managed to earn a profit in every year of the decade. With performance like this, Thor Industries could build up its family of companies, which kept getting larger. Since its founding in August 1980, Thor had acquired General Coach, Dutchmen Manufacturing, Four Winds International, Comfort Corporation, and Champion Bus Company. Airstream was now part of a large and important corporation with all the benefits and security that brings. Best of all, Airstream stood at the top of the corporate pyramid—it was Thor's crown jewel and everybody knew it. And yet, for Airstream, the best was yet to come.

ENTER CHRIS DEAM

In 2000, Riegel met industrial designer Christopher C. Deam, an incredibly talented designer and architect whose work interests included architecture, transportation, product design, and product innovation. Deam had approached Airstream with interior design ideas around 1996, but the company turned down his ideas as "not being for our audience." Later, Riegel was alerted to a special trailer display created by Deam for a furniture show and, suitably impressed, invited Deam to Airstream to create an exciting interior for a new trailer model.

Deam had strong opinions about how Airstream's interiors should look. He wasn't happy with the existing designs. "What I found was, you had this great streamlined aerodynamic modern exterior, and then you opened the door and it was like grandma's kitchen. There was a disconnect between the exterior and the interior. You approached the trailer and there was the magic promise of the future, and you walk in and it was like a log cabin on wheels". Deam soon came up with a fantastic design that was roomy, airy, and exceptionally modern. Airstream approved and started production on this

A popular trailer among young families was the 25' Safari, seen here hooked up to a 1999 Ford Explorer tow vehicle. This couple is preparing for an autumn weekend of leaf peeping.

The late 1990s also saw the popular Airstream Classic, such as the 1999 model shown here. With generous interior space and an appealing layout, this model's light earth colors help to give a feeling of warmth and roominess.

special model, dubbed the Airstream CCD (the designer's initials), in 2001. It soon became one of the most popular Airstream models.

In an interview with the *New York Times*, Deam revealed some of his design ideas for Airstream trailers, including:

> Some smart space-saving devices [such as] cutouts in the rounded sink area, rolling vertical doors. We use LED lighting, which uses less power, which is very critical when you are out on the road. We have what is called a split bathroom (a toilet and sink on one side of the hall and the shower on the other side) with thin accordion doors on either side you can use if you want to create one larger bathroom. You learn these little tricks. It's also a story about light and the luminosity of the reflections on the aluminum. When you put wooden cabinets in, it always felt slightly foreign.

When you see a Deam interior, it always looks just right.

A big part of Airstream CCD's appeal was its use of aluminum on the interior walls, exposing the modern material rather than covering it up. Deam's interior designs were so unusual, however, that adding them

to the trailer assembly process took time and effort to perfect. Working with aluminum is not easy because the metal dings and dents easily, so workers had to be trained in new procedures for installing the interiors. It all proved worthwhile, though, when buyers responded very well to the new product line.

While Airstream CCD was getting off the ground, Riegel, Thompson, and Orthwein were working on what would become Thor's largest acquisition ever—the purchase of Keystone RV, a large company in the RV industry that led the market in towable recreational vehicles. To those outside the company, this plan looked like a huge misstep: the RV market had started to slide in early 2000 and orders for new trailers were slowing down.

Then came the terrorist attacks of September 11. Overnight, the stock market went into a tailspin—and the RV market went along with it. Thompson and Orthwein began to have doubts about buying Keystone, but the company's board of directors and Riegel finally swayed them, and the deal was done. The $151 million purchase of Keystone and its extensive roster of brands brought

Cougar, Sprinter, Raptor, Montana, Springdale, Retreat, and many other brands into Thor Industries' stable.

Despite the ominous economic landscape of the early 2000s, the deal proved a brilliant one: from sales of $400 million in 2001, Keystone's volume grew to $1 billion by 2004. The acquisition of Keystone made Thor Industries the undisputed leader in the RV business.

REVIVING AIRSTREAM—AGAIN

Meanwhile, Airstream itself was in something of a rut. Sales were fair, but the recession following 9/11 had badly depleted the dealer network. The company needed to freshen some of its older products and also bring out new models to reignite interest in the brand.

Riegel and Huttle met in March 2002 to examine Airstream's problems and formulate a plan that could correct the dealer network's deficiencies as well as the company's product line. After some discussion, the two men settled on a two-pronged approach: one person would dedicate his efforts to rebuilding Airstream's retail distribution network, while the other rode herd on product development. After further discussion, the two came up with an unusual plan that they presented to the Thor Industries' board of directors.

Under the plan, Huttle would become chairman of Airstream, focusing on rebuilding the dealer network, a task that played into his skill set. Meanwhile, Riegel would take on the role of president and CEO of the firm, setting as

Left: Although comical, this ad for the 2003 Volkswagen gets a few things wrong. For one thing, since the VW is a front-wheel-drive car, it couldn't possibly lift its front end trying to pull any trailer, let alone an Airstream. More importantly, although the trailer is fairly big, the special Airstream construction makes it lighter than comparable trailers, and even this little Bug would be able to pull it.

Bottom: Brian Johnson, lead singer for the Australian rock band AC/DC, bought himself the new Safari Special Edition shown here. The Safari line, introduced in 1998, used a more European approach to interior design and furnishings, which Airstream management felt would appeal more to younger families.

CALL 866-314-9017

LUXURIOUS TOURING

When you drive an Airstream Touring Coach you'll feel as if you're in a luxury automobile; yet with a complete kitchen and bath, full interior headroom, and generous sleeping areas, you have fantastic on-the-road accommodations with park-it-anywhere convenience!

AIRSTREAM INTERSTATE

The newest Airstream motorhome is the Interstate, such as this 2005 model. Built on a Dodge Sprinter chassis, it features a raised roof cap for adequate headroom and, despite its short wheelbase, manages to fit in enough amenities for a small family.

his main task the development of new products. Thompson approved the plan and it went into effect.

Huttle had radical ideas for building a new dealer network. To him, the idea of returning to the old ways, where dealers could represent as many manufacturers as they wanted, had become passé. He'd met many small businessmen and investors who were enthusiastic about the Airstream brand and hoped to make it their main product line. If there was enough product available,

they were willing to sell Airstream as their featured product line, rather than combining cheaper brands with Airstream as a special, marquee-type sideline. A few motivated investors even vowed to make Airstream their sole product line, becoming exclusive dealers.

Realizing that a dealer who dedicates himself to a single brand always works harder to make it successful, Huttle saw that the day of small, undercapitalized dealers was over. But being an extraordinary dealer meant having

A companion to the Interstate, the Airstream Westfalia was built on a long-wheelbase Sprinter chassis. Comfortable for touring, the Interstate was not ideal for overnight sleeping. When they were introduced, Sprinters were assembled under Mercedes, Freightliner, and Dodge nameplates.

sufficient capital to do the job properly. Dingy little stores with a small product inventory simply wouldn't cut it anymore. Huttle wanted his new dealers to have plenty of capital, along with the willingness to invest in outstanding facilities and lots of inventory, which would make their businesses look and feel successful. Huttle remained close to his customers and realized that the one thing they wanted was a dealer who could take care of their needs, be it sales, service, financing, or parts support.

They didn't want to look at photographs or catalogs of the trailer they were interested in buying—they wanted to see it on the lot, ready to purchase. And when it came time for service or repairs, they wanted factory-trained mechanics who would do a good job, the first time, every time. This all pointed toward larger, more progressive dealers than had been operating in the past. All of this excited Huttle, and he was anxious to bring Airstream's retail network into the twenty-first century.

Right: The Land Yacht 31.

Below: A big Airstream Class A motorhome for 2005. Note the foldout awning on the side and slideout rear section.

A side by side comparison of the Interstate (left) and the Westfalia (right) shows the differences in wheelbase length, roof heights, and window shapes.

Huttle's planning worked exceedingly well. By 2005, he had added forty new dealers for the most part larger, stronger, and even more dedicated than the dealers who'd dropped out during the recession. Thanks to his efforts, the look and spirit of the Airstream retail group improved greatly over a short period of time.

As Huttle worked his magic on Airstream's retail operations, Riegel was tackling Airstream's product problems. Having Deam on board was a huge help: the designer was charged with going through the Airstream line and updating the interior trim with the goal of making Airstream the premier luxury trailer in the world. With his background in art and architecture, Riegel respected Deam, and they shared an understanding of which ideas would be the most successful.

The area of quality was another concern for Riegel. Industry standards were constantly improving. He knew that Airstream's redesigned products should also reflect the increased level quality demanded by the industry—it wouldn't do to fall behind.

In addition, Riegel wanted to build products that were faster, better, and less expensive. It was a tall order. As a Thor executive, Riegel had lived in New York; now, as Airstream's CEO, he would need to be much closer to the action. Riegel decided to take a page from Thompson's playbook and live in Ohio Monday through Friday, returning home to New York and family for the weekends.

To ensure that he had his fingers on the pulse of his operations, Riegel established his Jackson Center office in the middle of the plant, in a former second-floor storeroom. Windows were installed so he could keep an eye on the production floor, and also so that his employees could see him and know that he was right there, always available and working side by side with them. The new office proved to be a fairly noisy location, with all the clinging and clanging of a busy shop floor. As CEO, though, Riegel felt that the middle of the shop was where he belonged, so he stayed there. He maintained an open-door policy in which any employee could drop in to see him, a gesture appreciated by his workers.

The 9/11 terrorists attacks had a curious effect on Americans: they reignited and sharpened their love of country, encouraging them to vacation closer to home and see for themselves the vastness and beauty of their nation. Industry sales of travel trailers soared 21 percent in 2002, another 3 percent in 2003, and a solid 15 percent in 2004, greatly expanding the market. Airstream was ready to take advantage of this market growth with its new and updated products. The company was recognized as the second-fastest growing travel trailer brand in America in 2003 and 2004, which was surprising for a premium-priced vehicle offered by a mature company.

Top: Visitors to the Jackson Center service department of Airstream are familiar with the sight of the bay doors for the facility's large and well-equipped service garage. The entire history of Airstream, from 1932 to the present, might be here, receiving service from the best technicians in the business.

Bottom: Airstream celebrated its fiftieth year of manufacturing in 2002. To mark the occasion, the company held a big cookout for employees and retirees at its Ohio headquarters. Company managers honored those former and current workers by cooking and serving the meals themselves. Later, everyone gathered for this celebratory "family" photo.

Still, Airstream's upgraded product line, along with its heightened attention to product costs and quality, made it one of the big winners in the sales arena.

The Deam-designed International CCD was a big part of the reason for Airstream's success, spawning other CCD models. In time, the standard 23-foot International CCD was joined by 25-foot and 28-foot versions, as well as 16-foot and 19-foot Bambi CCDs, for a total of five CCD models. Together they accounted for a surprisingly large percentage of Airstream's sales volume.

In 2002, Airstream celebrated its fiftieth year in Ohio. It was a long way in miles and memories from where the company had started, in a little rented plant in Los Angeles, to the large, modern factory in Jackson Center. To mark the occasion, the company held a big cookout for employees and retirees, honoring them by having Airstream managers do all the cooking and serving.

Riegel proved a popular leader when he raised employees' pay and received approval to invest some $3 million to improve conditions at the plant in the form of new lighting, improved production tools and processes, and repaving the employee's parking lot. It all helped to maintain the outstanding employee relations always enjoyed by Airstream. Several times over the years, unions have come to Airstream seeking to unionize the shops, but each time their proposals have been turned down by workers who see little advantage in aligning with organized labor. After all, they already receive good pay and decent benefits, and they're treated well. They have had opportunities for advancement as well as reasonably secure employment. What more could a union offer workers except to place an unwanted layer of separation between them and the company?

By 2003, Riegel felt it was time to introduce more new product types. Daimler-Chrysler—the short-lived "union" of Daimler-Benz (builder of Mercedes-Benz vehicles) and Chrysler Corporation—had developed a large commercial van that seemed like the ideal platform for a new Airstream motorhome. As a work truck, the Mercedes-designed product was offered through Dodge dealers as the Dodge Sprinter, through Mercedes commercial dealers as the Mercedes Sprinter, and through Freightliner dealers as—no surprise—the Freightliner Sprinter. Now Airstream would modify its vans and offer them through their own dealer network.

The company initially built their new motorhome on the Dodge chassis; over time, though, they switched to the Mercedes nameplate. Called the Airstream Interstate, it is a Class B motor coach, initially seating six and offering sleeping accommodations for two. Powered by a rugged Mercedes-Benz diesel engine, the big coach attained fuel economy of a reported 22 miles per gallon, an outstanding result for such a large vehicle. Unlike many Class B motor coaches, the Airstream retains its original width, and the clever design has allowed for the inclusion of a full kitchen plus bath facilities in addition to its sleeping and passenger carrying capacity.

Over time, the Interstate has spawned other variations. The first was called the Sprinter Westfalia, set on a Dodge

A view inside the service department's comfortable waiting lounge. The couple seated here are longtime Airstream owners and veterans of many trips.

Video screen inside the Airstream customer waiting lounge. The entire interior of this comfy area is done up in aluminum sheet metal, just like Airstream trailers themselves.

chassis but with a completely different floor plan and roof design that allowed sleeping for four people.

The year 2004 also brought a new Airstream vehicle concept. The Airstream Skydeck Motorhome featured gorgeous wood and aluminum interior trim, black leather couches, and a set of stairs leading to a rooftop living area that boasted seating, tables, and umbrellas. Ideal for corporate events that require a fully equipped yet fully mobile building to accommodate guests, the Skydeck was perhaps the most exciting Airstream product yet. Corporate users included Coors Brewing Company, which brought one to the 2005 Super Bowl.

The company greatly expanded its workforce between 2002 and 2004, adding more than 180 new associates for a total of about 450 employees. These workers were needed because industry sales had continued to grow, with 2004's numbers the highest since 1980.

As sales continued to boom, Airstream management sought ways to boost production further, even though plant floor space was getting tighter by the day. The solution was to institute even leaner inventory practices than before,

freeing up floor space formerly used for holding materials so that it could be used for production. New machinery was also added to speed up processing while improving quality, such as computer-controlled routers and panel saws. For calendar year 2004, Airstream reported over $90 million in sales, a 70 percent increase in revenues.

Airstream welcomed Bob Wheeler as vice president of product development in 2004. He began his professional career at General Motors after receiving his MBA from the State University at New York in Buffalo and a BS in mechanical engineering from the University of Rochester. Wheeler had worked at Fleetwood before joining the Thor subsidiary Dutchmen Manufacturing, Inc. A tremendously dedicated individual, Wheeler would soon leave his mark on Airstream.

A SURPRISE ANNOUNCEMENT

Airstream and Thor Industries had a very good year for 2004, followed by another in 2005, when Airstream began selling its products in the UK and continental Europe. Then, on July 26, 2005, Thor issued a surprise announcement: a complete reorganization of its management team.

Thompson and Orthwein were pleased with Riegel's performance at Airstream—since 2002, he had doubled sales and increased profits tenfold. They promoted him to group president at Thor, which meant leaving Jackson Center and taking over US-based subsidiaries like Thor California, Komfort Corp, Crossroads RV, and

Breckenridge, along with Canadian firms General Coach Oliver, BC, and General Coach Hensall Ontario.

Taking Riegel's place at the head of Airstream in Jackson Center would be Wheeler, who hadn't been with the company long but had been with Thor for a number of years. He was the best choice to become Airstream's president and CEO. Huttle remained as chairman of Airstream, while Mark Wahl was elevated to senior vice

Airstream's 2015 Eddie Bauer model, offering a unique rear hatch to make access easier for pets and the various "toys" outdoor types like to bring with them, such as kayaks and canoes.

Four-footed friends? Welcome.

Traveling in an Eddie Bauer Airstream means never having to leave your best buddies behind. Pet-friendly features are standard – so dogs are always welcome.

• Extra-durable, stain-resistant Sunbrella™ upholstery helps this Airstream interior stand up to whatever your dogs dish out.

• Sturdy exterior tie-downs keep Rover from roving too far.

• A heavy-duty entry door guard keeps pets safely inside; protects screen door from scratching.

• A convenient hand-held outdoor shower is perfect for hosing off muddy paws.

president of operations. Thus Airstream remained in the hands of highly effective managers who knew the business well, an increasingly important factor as the decade progressed.

Since 2002, RV industry sales had been growing steadily: that year saw growth of 21.1 percent with 311,000 units shipped, followed by 3.2 percent growth in 2003, 15.4 percent in 2004, 3.9 percent in 2005, and finally 1.6 percent in 2006 with 390,000 RVs shipped to dealers. For the industry, it had been a phenomenal run, but now things were about to head in the opposite direction. A harsh recession was brewing and, because trailers and motorhomes are luxury, discretionary purchases, the RV industry was among the first to feel its sting. Airstream was not immune from the coming hardships.

THE GREAT RECESSION

It started slowly, with industry sales falling 9.5 percent in 2007. The next year, the financial crisis hit the US economy hard, devastating the RV industry with a devastating 32.9 percent slump, followed in 2009 by a further 30.1 percent drop. RV sales of 165,000 vehicles that year were less than half of what they had been in 2006. It was a disaster for all the businesses involved, and Airstream, being near the top of the industry price ladder, suffered as least as much as the other companies. In a later interview, Wheeler stated that, "since RVs are a big-ticket discretionary purchase industry, [the industry] got hammered and we were no exception. Oh-eight and oh-nine were pretty bad years."

During the recession, Airstream's business dropped by 60 percent. As sales slumped, the company's management

Life doesn't get much better than this!

was forced to address the problem. Because its products are essentially hand-built, a great deal of labor goes into their manufacture, which requires a lot of workers. With so few orders coming into the plant, the company was forced to slash its work force to match demand. It was an agonizing process, but before it was over roughly half of Airstream's workers were laid off. Bob Wheeler made a vow to them that, when the company returned to health, it would rehire every worker it had been forced to let go.

Wheeler decided to use the reduction in business as an opportunity to improve the manufacturing processes. The remaining workers were charged with finding new, faster ways to build Airstreams, all the while adhering to the principles of lean manufacturing. Wheeler knew that if they could fine-tune the build process, it would pay off in a big way during slow times as they waited for the inevitable upturn in business.

The wait was only a few years: the country had begun the slow process of recovery by 2010. Wheeler made good on his vow, rehiring every worker who wanted to come back.

Before the return of business health, though, sad news arrived on November 12, 2009, when Wade Thompson, the man who had saved Airstream, passed away at his home in Manhattan from complications of colon cancer. At the time of his death he was sixty-nine years old, still energetic, still enthusiastic about the recreational vehicle business. The entire Thor family mourned his passing.

RECOVERY

The economic recovery was dramatic when it happened. In 2011 alone, Airstream sales shot up 175 percent, with unit sales of trailers doubling and motor coaches showing a strong increase as well. That year, the Airstream Interstate became the top-selling Class B motor coach in the United States. A year later, Airstream was building at a rate of about twenty-seven trailers a week, in addition to five vans. RV industry sales climbed 13.2 percent in 2012 and 2.4 percent in 2013. Airstream, Inc.'s numbers for the same period continued to improve as well.

The company's dealer network had also grown to sixty-five dealers with five in Canada. As Bob Wheeler noted, though, "they're not distributed evenly. We have

a lot of dealers in key markets like Southern California and California in general." He felt the company was underrepresented in certain parts of the country and vowed to correct the situation. Most of Airstream's dealers were still multibrand outlets, though a small number handled Airstream exclusively.

Airstream's parent company received a shock in 2012 when Riegel, now senior group president, announced he was quitting the firm to start a new company of his own. Riegel had come up with a vision for a new kind of travel business, which he called Airstream 2 Go. His plan was to rent current-model Airstream trailers and proper tow vehicles to consumers and commercial customers. The company would also offer complete travel planning services and support. Riegel's resignation from Thor was effective September 30, though he continued as a consultant into the next year. Airstream 2 Go opened for business in May 2013.

By 2014, the Jackson Center plant had run out of space again, with production having risen to fifty travel trailers per week, plus Interstate motor coaches produced in the old bazooka factory building across the street from the main plant. The company had set records three years in a row: its order backlog for trailers was running about three months, with shipments at twice the rate they had been before the Great Recession. By this point, management realized that a major plant expansion was essential, and plans were laid for building enough new floor space to accommodate a 50 percent increase in production capacity. Industry sales in October 2014 were the best they had been in forty years, and they were still increasing. The existing factory's expansion was expected to be completed in May 2015.

NEW DESIGNS AND LINEUPS

As part of a new strategy to revitalize product design, Airstream worked with the Columbus College of Art and Design to plan and build a camper featuring a combination of work space and living area. The new concept, aimed at people whose jobs allow them to live and work anywhere, is expected to influence the design of future Airstream vehicles.

This interior belongs to a 2015 Airstream Flying Cloud, one of the company's most popular models. Generous seating room and a stylish rounded kitchen sink are just two of this trailer's compelling features. Note the overhead lighting as well.

The smallest Airstream currently in production, the Sport, replaces the Bambi. Although the Bambi nameplate is no longer in use, any single-axle Airstream is usually referred to as a Bambi.

CHAPTER SEVEN

AIRSTREAM TODAY

For many years, Airstream has been the largest employer in little Jackson Center, Ohio. From its big main plant on West Pike Street, where travel trailers are manufacturered, to the smaller Interstate motor coach plant across the street in the former bazooka plant, Airstream dominates downtown Jackson Center. Down the street from the plant is the world headquarters of the Wally Byam Caravan Club International. Vehicles fill the street, some still being assembled, most ready for shipment.

The company is also the oldest travel trailer brand in America, the simple result of outlasting its competitors. Back in 1932, shortly after Wally began producing his early trailers in a factory, there had been fewer than 48 trailer manufacturers registered for business in the United States. Five years later, that number had grown to more than 400 American manufacturers. Of all those companies, Airstream alone survives. Kozy Coach, Spartan Trailers, Covered Wagon—they're all long gone. Others have come to take their place, but Airstream alone has endured.

Airstream is not only alive, it is thriving as never before. And for that we can thank Wally Byam because it was his determination, and sheer stubborness, that kept Airstream afloat. That, along with a succession of gutsy, hard-working managers, product planners, engineers, and product

designers. And let's not forget the assembly crafters, the men and women who create Airstream trailers out of raw materials that flow into the plant in a never ending stream. We've watched them as they take wood, aluminum, fiberglass, and other materials and turn them into beautiful cabinets, bathrooms, countertops and ceilings. We sat amazed as they sawed, sewed, and hammered, and riveted

Opposite: Today, Airstream Interstate Touring Coaches are produced in the former main factory building in Jackson Center, Ohio, originally a bazooka plant during World War II. It is a beehive of activity.

Top: Using a long-wheelbase Mercedes-Benz Sprinter commercial chassis, the new Interstate features modern bus-style windows for outstanding visibility.

Inside, the Interstate features an ultra-plush interior with all the amenities one could want.

each and every one of the thousands of parts that go into an Airstream trailer. It's a sight to see.

Airstream continues as the proud flagship brand of RV industry leader Thor Industries. Peter Orthwein, Thor's surviving cofounder, continues as executive chairman of the board, while young and talented Robert W. Martin serves as president and CEO. In 2014, the company did over $3.5 billion in sales and reported a net profit of $470 million. It's a large, efficient, and successful corporation. Wade Thompson would be proud. Out of hopes and dreams—and very little cash— he and Orthwein created an enduring corporation, one of the best-managed companies in America.

Bob Wheeler, president of Airstream, Inc. since August 1, 2005, continues to build his plants' production capacity to accommodate the ever-growing demand for new Airstream travel trailers. As of summer 2015, the Airstream factories comprise about 200,000 square feet

and the company employs some 574 people. In certain job classifications, Airstream has one problem that most companies don't have to face in our time—a shortage of workers. The company maintains a constant search for engineers and marketing specialists with the appropriate certifications and degrees.

At the time of this writing the company was producing about seventy-five trailers per week, an amazing record considering the size, complexity, and cost of these vehicles, but demand is strong and continues to grow.

One thing that *is* discussed whenever Airstream executives get together is whether or not the company should get back into building Class A motorhomes. Just about everybody agrees they'd love to do it, but the ramp up to production of these new vehicles would call for a completely new design, then a further investment in building a new production facility; there isn't a square foot of available space at the Jackson Center main plant

On a 2015 visit to the Airstream headquarters and factory campus, the author saw this lineup of historic trailers parked in front of the Customer Service Lounge. The gold one is a famous unit that once belonged to Wally and Stella Byam.

or the old bazooka plant. Stay tuned—customer demand may one day force the issue. There is a lot of nostalgia for the Airstream motorhome.

Since hitting a rough patch during the Great Recession, the company's network of retail dealers has grown to fifty-seven dealer outlets in the United States, ten of which handle Airstream products exclusively. There are also six dealers in Canada, and seven in the rest of the world, including a new one in China. While this sales coverage is impressive, there is plenty of room for further expansion of the worldwide network. Overseas demand is growing at least as fast as in the United States—and why not? No one else in the world makes a product to compare with the classic Airstream.

So what should we take away from this story of Airstream? What can we learn from the Airstream legacy? Maybe we can answer these questions with Wally's wisdom, spoken more than fifty-five years ago on his way to the hospital.

A concerned caravaner asked Wally, almost childlike, what they all should do while he was in the hospital. Wally didn't hesitate. He replied,

> Don't stop. Keep right on going. Hitch up your trailer and go to Canada or down to Old Mexico. Head for Europe, if you can afford it, or go to the Mardi Gras. Go someplace you've heard about, where you can fish or hunt or collect rocks or just look up at the sky. Find out what's at the end of some country road. Go see what's over the next hill, and the one after that, and the one after that.

That, dear friends, is wisdom for the ages. May we always follow it!

Starting at the bottom of this outstanding aerial photo, we can see a group of Airstream trailers parked, probably gathered for an Alumapalooza meet. The large blue building with the white roof is the main plant where trailers are produced, along with most of their interior components. Moving up and to the left, a smaller blue building fronts the main road: this is the Service Department and Customer Waiting Lounge. Directly across the street is another large building, the old bazooka plant, which now produces Interstate motor coaches.

INDEX

ABOUT THE AUTHOR

Patrick R. Foster is one of America's best-known automotive journalists who has been writing for more than twenty-five years. His work has appeared in *Hemmings Classic Car*, *AutoWeek*, *Automobile Quarterly*, *Automotive News*, *Collectible Automobile*, and other periodicals. Foster has regular columns in *Hemmings Classic Car* and *Old Cars Weekly*.

He has written twenty books, including *American Motors Corporation: The Rise and Fall of America's Last Independent Automaker*, *Jeep: The History of America's Greatest Vehicle*, and *International Harvester Trucks: The Complete History*.

He has contributed material to several other books as well. Foster has won numerous writing awards, including the Lee Iacocca Award, perhaps the most coveted award in the old car hobby, for excellence in automotive writing. The 2015 International Automotive Media Council Awards saw him bring home a Silver Medal for an article on the 1930–1934 Nash automobiles, and a bronze medal for his book *Jeep: The History of America's Greatest Vehicle*.